# The Development of Sociomoral Knowledge
*A Cognitive-Structural Approach*

# THE
# DEVELOPMENT
# OF
# SOCIOMORAL
# KNOWLEDGE

*A Cognitive-Structural Approach*

## HUGH ROSEN

COLUMBIA UNIVERSITY PRESS
New York
1980

LIBRARY OF CONGRESS CATALOGING IN PUBLICATION DATA

ROSEN, HUGH.
   THE DEVELOPMENT OF SOCIOMORAL KNOWLEDGE.

   BIBLIOGRAPHY: P.
   INCLUDES INDEX.
   1. MORAL DEVELOPMENT.   2. SOCIALIZATION.
3. COGNITION IN CHILDREN.   4. KOHLBERG, LAWRENCE,
1927–    5. PIAGET, JEAN, 1896–    I. TITLE.
[DNLM: 1. MORALS.   2. SOCIAL VALUES.   3. COGNITION.
HM216 R813D]

BF723.M54R67     155.2'34     80-20
ISBN 0-231-04998-6
ISBN 0-231-04999-4 PBK.

COLUMBIA UNIVERSITY PRESS
NEW YORK   GUILDFORD, SURREY

*To*
## Michael Pauling
*whose relentless quest for justice in this world
has been variously an irritant and an inspiration*

# Contents

# Acknowledgments

My special thanks to Dr. Martin Whiteman, psychologist and professor at the Columbia University School of Social Work, for introducing me to the field of cognitive development through his brilliant course on Piaget. I am also appreciative of the light-handed but challenging manner in which he engaged me in discussions on Kohlberg's moral developmental system when he served as my dissertation adviser as I prepared an earlier version of this manuscript.

I would like to recognize a debt to my friends and colleagues of the Biomedical Ethics section in the Department of Mental Health Sciences at the Hahnemann Medical College in Philadelphia. Their sustained interest and anticipation of this work generated uplifting momentum that was most helpful.

Certainly the students at Hahnemann to whom I have taught much of the material in this book over the years deserve to be recognized. Their enthusiastic interest has propelled my own toward an upward spiral. Their incisive questions have contributed to my attempts to impose increasing order and clarity upon the material. Most importantly, they have convinced me that the commitment to grappling with the moral issue of justice is as great today as it has ever been.

A special note of thanks goes to my secretary, Mrs. Barbara Cunningham, who graciously bore up under my mounting anxiety with the passage of time throughout the preparation of this book.

Lastly, I wish to express my gratitude to Dr. Vicki Raeburn, associate executive editor at the Columbia University Press. Her personal vigor and confidence in this book sustained me during many months of eager anticipation.

# Introduction

The exposition of this book is concerned with the development of sociomoral knowledge. In this prelude, I wish simply to provide an orientation to the organization of the material. Each of the succeeding chapters is an amplification of these few introductory comments. Although they may be read in isolation, the sequence of chapters builds a hierarchy of knowledge which reflects the character of the very subject of the book. Therefore, maximum comprehension and appreciation are likely to follow from reading the chapters in order.

Because of the very nature of this subject area there is an inherent logic which strongly urges a particular approach. The theoretical underpinnings of sociomoral knowledge are rooted in cognitive developmental psychology, which emphasizes stages, interaction, adaptation, structure, differentiation, integration, hierarchy, and equilibration. Therefore, a general presentation of the theoretical foundation of cognitive-structural development is essential. This is also a requirement for comprehending sociomoral development because specific stages of such development cannot be achieved without the presence of the appropriately corresponding cognitive period, although the presence of any cognitive period does not assure a corresponding level of moral development.

Although this book is not exclusively on the work of a single theorist, the central figure is Lawrence Kohlberg, the leading contemporary moral developmentalist. His work draws heavily upon Jean Piaget's genetic epistemology in general, as outlined in the first chapter, and specifically upon Piaget's only book on moral development, which is discussed in the second chapter. The influences are unmistakable and a scholarly grasp of Kohlberg demands an acquaintance with the earlier theorist's research and observations on moral development, first published in 1932.

Similarly to what has been stated above in relation to cognitive-structural development, the construction of social knowledge is also a necessary, but not sufficient condition for moral reasoning. Egocentrism, the inability to take another's point of view, is present in varying forms at each level of development. As egocentrism at one level declines, a step forward is evident in the developing child's ability to take another's point of view. This increasing capacity for perspective undergoes qualitative advances in development as each new form of egocentrism is conquered. In order to adequately reason morally at any given level of a Kohlbergian stage, the corresponding stage of role-taking ability must be achieved. It follows logically, therefore, that one cannot fully comprehend moral development without a knowledge of the acquisition of social role-taking skills and structures. The work of Mead, Flavel, Feffer, and Selman will be examined in chapter 3 to provide the necessary orientation to this area.

The areas of cognitive development and role-taking ability logically dovetail into a full exposition of Kohlberg's highly researched position on moral development in chapter 4. The six universal stages are examined in depth. Both their philosophical and psychological foundations are explained. The developing nature of the "justice structure" is analyzed.

There are several major themes that dominate the literature on Kohlberg's research and these are examined at some length in chapter 5. These themes are as follows: the relationship between moral stage and action, the hierarchical nature of moral stages, and the relationship between moral and cognitive development.

In chapter 6 a critique is presented of Kohlberg's methodology and theoretical position. I have attempted in the chapter to do justice to the serious criticisms that have appeared in various quarters. Therefore I have avoided offering point by point rebuttals on Kohlberg's behalf. In a very real sense, all of the chapters preceding the criticism constitute a response.

The final chapter takes a pragmatic turn. Various perspectives on intervention are described. Interventive theories and practices at psychodynamic, interpersonal, and organizational levels are examined. Helping professionals carry a responsibility for vigilance to emerging knowledge that might prove beneficial in attempts to understand and assist those who are being served. It is the author's belief that the sociomoral developmental system of Kohlberg, based upon Piaget's constructivist psychology, is greatly relevant to achieving clinical goals: the client's development and enhanced interpersonal relationships. Therefore, the scope of the Piaget-Kohlberg model is presented through a conceptual organization that I hope the reader will find both personally and professionally meaningful. Comprehension of the model has the potential for transforming what we do and how we view it.

The Development of Sociomoral Knowledge
*A Cognitive-Structural Approach*

# Chapter One

# A Cognitive-Structural
# Foundation

## STRUCTURALISM AND EPISTEMOLOGY

⟨The work of Lawrence Kohlberg, the heart of this book, pulsates within the body of cognitive-structural developmental psychology. To understand Kohlberg's contribution to sociomoral knowledge in depth, it is necessary that one be familiar with the historical and theoretical framework which encases it.⟩In this chapter I will present salient aspects of the epochal work of Jean Piaget (1896–    ), from which Kohlberg has drawn so freely in pursuing his own innovative findings. The following chapter will concentrate exclusively on Piaget's theory of moral development, since it has served as the point of departure for Kohlberg's investigations into that field.

⟨ Both Piaget and Kohlberg adopt a theoretical position known as structuralism. A structuralist approach cuts across disciplines and has been applied to such wide-ranging areas as mathematics, biology, anthropology, sociology, linguistics, and literature.⟩ Two major sources on the subject of structuralism, Piaget's *Structuralism* and Gardner's *Quest for Mind,* offer useful expositions which identify its essentials.⟨Structuralism is a method of analyzing and understanding phenomena rather than a dogma of content. The structuralist scans the surface manifestations of things or events and penetrates below these to grasp the underlying order and significance which form a meaningful pattern. The superficial detail and diversity that appear on the surface prove to be less significant than the coherent pattern of the deep structures which give rise to what is overtly perceived.] The submerged patterned relationships of whatever is under consideration are what constitute the sources of reality and account for observed regularities, rather than the atomized surface details. Emphasis is placed upon the self-regulating system of relationships and transformations among the interdependent elements comprising the totality or whole of a phenomenon.]

Prominent among modern structuralists are Noam Chomsky, a linguist, and Claude Lévi-Strauss, an anthropologist. Both believe in the existence of deep universal structures within the human organism which account for formal patterned regularities in language and cultural behaviors, despite the manifest variation of peoples across the world and through time. However congenial this outlook may appear to be to the work of Jean Piaget, the Geneva genius breaks sharply from it on one extremely vital issue. The theories of Chomsky and Lévi-Strauss are agenetic. They do not deal with the genesis of those underlying structures which govern behavior. Piaget, to the contrary, sees the emergence of structures deriving from a continual process of construction. This process is autoregulated and is promoted by the organism's interaction with its environment.

Piaget is a genetic epistemologist before all else. Regardless of how valuable his contribution may be to developmental psychology, his own avowed primary aim has been to study the nature of knowledge and its origins. He chose to work with children because approaching his goal this way seemed to be the best means for achieving it. The work of Piaget and of what has become known as his Geneva school is set apart from that of the famous epistemological philosophers who preceded him in that it rests upon extensive research. This is true despite the sometimes intimidating features of its theoretical components. In effect, he introduced a scientific approach to epistemology, with an emphasis upon the development of knowledge in each individual from birth through adolescence. Piaget has attempted to avoid the pitfalls of either empiricism or rationalism which great thinkers in the tradition of Western philosophy had previously fallen into. Rationalists such as Plato, Spinoza, and Leibnitz formulated theories of knowledge which denied sensory experience as a source of reality. Instead they identified a priori mental activity divorced from sensory data as the true mode of acquiring knowledge. In fact, those familiar with Plato's illustration of the cave will recall that he went so far as to characterize sensorial impressions as having distracting and distorting effects upon the epistemic subject. Embracing the empiricist tradition in epistemology are such theorists as Locke, Berkeley, and Hume, each of whom stressed the role of sensory experience in the acquisition of knowledge. Locke rejected the notion of innate ideas and likened the mind to a blank slate which receives impressions from experience in the environment, the ultimate source of ideas. Simple ideas thus derived from sensory data are combined into aggregates of complex ideas. These complex ideas do not follow in their formation any predetermined pattern. of organization or sequence. In the work of Kant we find an attempt to reconcile these two divergent orientations to epistemological theorizing. While acknowledging a contribution to knowledge of sensory experience, Kant maintained that we do not come to know objective reality as it exists independently of the knowing subject. The explanation for this assertion resides in his contention that we have certain a priori intuitions and categories of mind which restructure and impose meaning upon the incoming data. Conceptions of time, space, and causality, for example, are innate to the human mind and these assure that experience will be ordered and processed in a particular way, exclusive of any alternative possibilities. The emphasis upon the knowing subject actively participating in construing knowledge from his experience justifies characterizing Kant as an intellectual forerunner of Piaget. In a later chapter we will see that Kant also plays a significant role in Kohlberg's theory of moral development. However, as with Chomsky and Lévi-Strauss, Piaget makes a concentrated effort to differentiate his epistemological position from that of Kant's in one major respect. Piaget thoroughly rejects any notion of innate ideas or structures. Yet this in no way brings him into the empiricist camp.

Piaget is a radical constructivist who posits the continuous development of new structures out of old ones which become more complexly organized into increasingly adaptive superordinate structures. Emergent cognitive structures usher in qualitatively different ways of thinking. Intellectual development is not a simple matter of quantitative increase in intelligence. Young children comprehend reality in ways that are qualitatively different from those in middle childhood, who in turn comprehend reality differently from adolescents. The child's cognitive developmental level, therefore, confers meaning upon experience, while at the same time limiting the scope and depth of that meaning.

What is a structure? Kohlberg explicitly states, "Structure refers to the general characteristic of shape, pattern, or organization of response rather than to the rate or intensity of response or its pairing with particular stimuli." In elaborating further, he goes on to say, ". . . 'cognitions' are internally organized wholes or systems of internal relations, that is, structure. Cognitive structures are rules of processing information or for connecting experienced events."[1] The developing changes which structures undergo comprise the stage theory in Piaget's work, which shall now be examined.

## THE FUNCTIONAL INVARIANTS

In contrast to structures, which undergo qualitative changes throughout development, functions remain the same regardless of age or stage. Piaget has posited two functional invariants, which are characteristic of all living organisms. These functions are organization and adaptation. Because of his employment of these functions in his theory of cognitive development, Piaget's conception of human intelligence is understood to be rooted in a biological model. In adopting this framework, Piaget avoids the split between mind and body to be found in Cartesian dualism. For Piaget, human intelligence is simply a subset of biological functioning.

Organization is essentially an internal affair in which more basic cognitive structural elements are integrated into hierarchical systems of relationships. This occurs with increasing complexity throughout development. A simple example is the coordination during infancy of grasping and visual activities, which earlier had been functioning in isolation from one another. The ability to coordinate these two activities derives from the organization of the previously separated structures that govern them. Later in development many more complex instances will emerge, such as the integration of classification and seriation structures to form a cognitive system promoting the comprehension of number.

Adaptation is an external matter in its emphasis upon the organism's interaction with the environment. It is comprised of two aspects, assimilation and accommodation, which are both present in varying degrees in all mental activity. Assimilation is a conservative force which leads to interpreting reality in terms of the present level of structural development. Hence, preschool children presented with a set of twelve wooden beads, ten brown ones and two white ones, will answer that there are more brown beads when asked whether there are more brown or more wooden beads. Told to restate the question, they indicate a belief that they had been asked whether there were more brown beads than white beads. Because they have not yet developed classification structures providing an understanding of a relationship between a whole and its subparts, they distort the question by assimilating it to their present level of understanding only single classes. Once they have developed cognitive structures providing understanding of hierarchical classification systems, assimilation of the question will not lead to distortion but to accurate comprehension. Accommodation, on the other hand, is a progressive component in that it induces structural change to meet the demands of what is new and novel in the environment. A very young child who has a globular cognitive structure which classifies all moving objects endowed with fur as a "doggie" will eventually differentiate the structure to accommodate the diversity of furry animals he will inevitably encounter.

Adaptation and organization continue to function in the same invariant manner as structural changes occur during the various developmental sequences.

## DEVELOPMENTAL STAGES AND PERIODS

Cognitive structural development progresses in an unvarying sequence. In the passage from one stage to the next, lower-order structures are integrated into a higher-order system of structural wholes. The rate of progress will vary from individual to individual, as well as from culture to culture. The demands of the environment and the nature of personal experience undergone by the interacting organism within it will greatly affect this rate of cognitive development. However, according to Piaget there is an inherent logic to cognitive-structural development which does not permit deviation from the sequence with which structures are found to evolve. Therefore, although general age trends can be identified in development, age cannot reliably be utilized as a predictive measure of stage in any given individual. On the other hand, knowing the stage that an individual is at does serve as a predictive tool in determining what cognitive competencies are at his command. To know what stage a child is capable of performing at, the investigator must make a cognitive diagnosis of that particular child.

Piaget's assertion of the universality of stages is sometimes misinterpreted to mean that all people will pass through all stages. The achievement of arriving at the final stage of cognitive development is by no means assured. All that can be accurately predicted from the theory is that anyone who has progressed to a certain point will have followed the same sequence of development as anyone else who has reached that same point.

☞ There are four periods of development formulated in Piaget's work, each one marking a major qualitative advance over the child's previous way of knowing the world. Piaget has concentrated primarily upon the child's construction of knowledge regarding the physical world. In more recent years, while Piaget's efforts continue in the same direction, there has been an intensive surge of activity attempting to extend his cognitive-developmental approach to social and moral domains. The interrelatedness of all these efforts will become increasingly manifest in the course of the present work.

The developmental periods presented below will concentrate upon essential characteristics. They have been elaborated upon by Piaget in innumerable works throughout a professional career extending over sixty years. Often he has devoted entire books to an exposition concentrating on only one period or cognitive dimension. Fortunately there exists a fairly recent and concise summary by Piaget and Inhelder, *The Psychology of the Child,* and in addition there is now available for the first time a comprehensive anthology of his work by Gruber and Vonèche, *The Essential Piaget.*

### The Sensorimotor Period

The sensorimotor period covers the stages of infancy ranging from birth to approximately eighteen months to two years. At birth the child exists in a virtual state of radical egocentrism. He experiences everything in his small universe as an extension of his own body and yet he completely lacks any sense of self. There is no distinction made between perceptual sensations and the stimuli in the environment from which they derive. Entering the world without any innate cognitive structures and equipped only with such primitive reflexes as sucking, grasping, and looking, the infant swiftly begins to explore his world. Gradually he begins to differentiate between his own body and that which exists beyond it.

The origins of intelligence as viewed by Piaget reside in the sensorimotor period. He has documented six stages of development constituting this period leading to representational thought. His comments upon these stages have been conceptualized into specific areas within which the infant is said to construct a knowledge of reality on a behavioral plane. The areas encompass means-end behavior, object permanence, causality, space, and time. Observation of the developing infant reveals increasingly more coordinated, complex, adaptive behaviors culminating in the emergence of representational thought in the sixth stage, the cognitive ability to represent mentally that which is absent from perception. Lastly, the child is no longer solipsistic, now demonstrating a behavioral comprehension of his position as one object relative to a multiplicity of others with none being the sole and fixed center around which the others revolve.

## The Preoperational Period

The preoperational period extends roughly from two years to six or seven years. It is generally divided into the preconceptual phase (two to four years) and the intuitive phase (four to seven years). Emphasis has been upon the cognitive limitations of this period and it is traditionally construed as a preparatory period paving the way for the emergence of systematic logical thinking in the concrete operational period. A growing trend, however, has been in the direction of identifying the positive achievements of this period. In any event, some of the most appealing aspects of child development occur during these preschool years, as reported in the early work of Piaget.

Although the youngster enters this period with the capability for representational thought, his thinking is unsystematic and subject to contradictions which have no unsettling effect upon him at all. In the preconceptual phase the child's concepts lack stability. They are characterized by neither true individuality nor true generality. Separate objects which are of the same class and are observed at different times are often mistaken as identical. At the same time, the preconceptual child does not conserve identity of an individual. A superficial change, such as putting on different clothing, can lead the child to conclude that a new individual has appeared. The later preoperational child does conserve identity and has acquired stability of single-class concepts, but cannot yet comprehend a hierarchy of classes.

Preoperational thought is perceptually bound. The child tends to center upon one salient aspect of a reality, while failing to simultaneously take into account other aspects as well. His thinking lacks reversibility, hence he can follow a process moving in one direction, but he cannot mentally retrace the steps in a reverse sequence to return to the starting point. Lastly, he cannot attend to transformational processes, but instead centers only upon beginning and end states of a process he may observe. All of these cognitive limitations are evidenced in the classic example of the preoperational child's inability to recognize the conservation of liquid poured from a short, wide beaker into a tall, thin one. Observing the pouring action, the child concludes that there is now more liquid in the second beaker because the water level is higher than it had been in the shorter beaker. He cannot decenter to realize that the gain in height has been reciprocally compensated for in the transformation by a loss in width. He cannot undergo a mental operation negating the action, which would provide him with an assurance that the amount of liquid has remained the same.

The concept of egocentrism is central to Piaget's entire system. What Piaget means by this rich and varied concept is the individual's inability to differentiate between subject and object. The egocentric knower does not distinguish between self and other. All of development may be seen as a series of conquests, at each major period, of the limitations imposed by egocentrism. Of particular relevance is the form of egocentrism during the preoperational period in which the knower is so embedded in his own perspective that he does not realize that the other may have an alternate, possibly even opposing, perspective. In chapter 3 I will elaborate upon this aspect of development at considerable length. Egocentrism is also prevalent among preoperational thinkers in relation to the inanimate world. The child does not conceive of events occurring by chance and instead he ascribes psychological motives to natural events.

## The Concrete Operational Period

The emergence of concrete operational thinking brings the rigor of genuine logic to the developing child. Although he is not consciously aware of it, his thinking is now governed by a rich interlocking network of systematically organized cognitive structures. Thought processes no longer occur in isolation from one another and this fact contributes significantly to the elimination of contradictory explanations. Piaget has drawn from the fields of logic and mathematics to formulate a set of nine models, which he calls groupings, that form a cognitive unconscious promoting the advances of this period. As with each cognitive epoch, however, there is a serious limitation. The logical thought of this period can only be carried out upon concrete objects either presently perceived in the environment or, in some cases, manipulated through mental representation. In either case the operational activity is confined to the familiar and known; it cannot be carried out on a highly abstract and purely hypothetical plane.

Piaget's logico-mathematical models are not ethereal constructions of Piaget's own mind or unrelated to the activities of the child. In fact, he derived them only after countless investigations of children's cognitive performances and through analysis of the explanations proffered by them to account for their own actions. It is Piaget's contention that the mode of information processing exhibited by the children studied appeared as if it flowed from the models he devised. The most significant areas explored in relation to this period involved tasks of conservation, classification, seriation, number, and transitivity.

Concrete operational thought is decentered, enabling the child to take into account more than one perspective at a time. For example, in the liquid conservation task, the child coordinates the transformation occurring between height and width, hence arriving at the conclusion that the amount remains the same despite the change that has occurred. Similarly, he is able to mentally reverse the act of pouring, which enables him to grasp that the amount is conserved since it would be the same were it to be poured back into the original container. In addition, the child has also constructed an identity operation, which imparts knowledge that since nothing has been added and nothing has been taken away, the amount must be the same despite the change in appearance after the liquid has been poured.

Reversible thinking is a cornerstone in Piaget's system. Its achievement in the concrete operational period, already cited in the conservation task, is clearly manifest in the areas of classification and seriation. In classification it takes the form of negation. The child now has the mobility of thought to realize not only that two subparts can be combined to produce a superordinate class, but also to reverse the procedure by subtracting one of the parts from the whole class to get the remaining part. Hence, for example, not only do triangles combined with squares yield a rectilinear class, but triangles subtracted from the rectilinear class will produce squares. It is precisely because he can decenter and perform the mental operation of negation or inversion that the concrete operational youngster does understand class inclusion.

Competence at seriation involves the type of reversibility known as reciprocity. Seriation invokes the ability to comprehend the relationships between a series of gradations ordered in a systematic progression from smallest or least intense to largest or most intense. Given a set of ten sticks, each a different size, the concrete operational thinker decenters as he grasps the reciprocal relationship in which $B$ is greater than $A$, but smaller than $C$, $D$, etc. Reciprocity is also present in that as $B$ is recognized as greater than $A$, reciprocally A is recognized as less than $B$.

It is on the basis of the preceding material and a variety of related experiments that Piaget constructed the complex logico-mathematical models of the concrete operational period. Although they will not be elaborated upon here, Flavell offers a commendable exposition of the models in his classic text on Piaget's work, *The Developmental Psychology of Jean Piaget*.

In summary, thinking during this period has become freed from the perceptual rootedness of preoperational thought. It is now decentered, transformational, and reversible. These attributes derive from mental operations which are interrelated systems of interiorized actions. Cognitive acts no longer are carried out in isolation and this fact eliminates the tendency toward contradictory statements existing side by side. Although capable of rigorous logical thought, the child's thinking is egocentric in that it is limited to the familiar objects of his everyday world.

## The Formal Operational Period

The formal operational period represents the fullest flowering of cognitive development in the Piagetian system. It generally reaches its threshold at about eleven or twelve years, but does not become stabilized until fourteen or fifteen. Currently it is being suggested that this period may be subdivided into two parts. The scope of the formal operational thinker is broadened to encompass the full range of the possible, with reality being merely one subset of this. Mental operations are no longer confined to familiar concrete objects in the environment, but are free to soar throughout the hypothetical universe. Where previously the objects of thought were those known things in the environment, now one's own thought becomes the object of thought. Instead of using only single propositions to make a statement about reality, such as "This ball is red," formal operational thought is interpropositional, hence deals with the logical relations between two propositions irrespective of reality. In elaborating upon this point Flavell states, "The less mature mind looks only to the *factual* relation between one proposition and the empirical reality to which it refers; the more mature mind looks also or instead to the *logical* relation between one proposition and another."[2] Interpropositional reasoning may be completely detached from any content and, hence, is purely formal. For example, one type of logical relation takes the form that if $x$ is present then $y$ is present, but that if $y$ is present then it does not follow that $x$ is present. This is a type of causality known as implication. A variation of this example is a causal relationship called reciprocal implication, which states that if $x$, then $y$, and if $y$, then $x$. These are cases of pure formal reasoning. It makes no difference what $x$ and $y$ refer to. The logical relationships involved are two of many possible types. They may or may not prove to be true when tested out upon actual objects in the real environment. Confronted with a set of materials and the problem of discovering cause and effect relationships, the formal operational thinker can invoke hypothetical deductive reasoning to resolve the problem. He utilizes the scientific method of developing an hypothesis and then proceeding to test it out by holding all variables constant except one, to observe its effect. He performs this systematically with each variable.

Piaget has designed two powerful models to explain formal operational thinking. One is the sixteen binary operations model. It is comprised of sixteen possible types of causal relationships which can logically be derived between two propositions. Implication and reciprocal implication are two of those possibilities and there exist fourteen others. The other model advanced by Piaget to account for formal operational thought is the INRC structure. It is a highly integrated cognitive structuration of what has preceded in development. The operations of INRC (identity, negation, reciprocity, and correlation) are all defined in relation to each other. It is only at the formal operational period that the young person fully understands the subtlety and multiplicity of these interrelated connections and is able to apply this comprehension across a wide range of problems. The extraordinary complexity of these models does not warrant further amplification here, but the interested reader may be rewarded by pursuing it in the work of Flavell.

It should be understood that in Western countries only about 50 percent of adults attain the formal operational period. Further, even those who have arrived at this period do not always function with it. Indeed, many of the demands of everyday life can be met adequately with the use of concrete operational thinking. Piaget, in "Intellectual Evolution from Adolescence to Adulthood," has recently raised the question of the generality of formal operations across all contents by those individuals possessing the necessary structural development. Theoretically, precisely because they deal with form and not content, the operational should have wide-ranging applicability across all areas. Piaget has acknowledged, however, that the individual's aptitudes and professional specializations influence the content areas to which he will be likely to apply formal operational thinking.

## THE EQUILIBRATION MODEL

Piaget's conception of intelligence is essentially one of adaptation. The human organism interacting with its environment strikes a proper balance between assimilation and accommodation to achieve adaptive intelligence. However, since structures are not innate, the existing cognitive structures at any given time are frequently encountering experiences in the environment which they cannot adequately cope with. At the point of such an encounter a disequilibrium occurs that results in a structural modification, ultimately a reorganization to a higher level of cognitive structuration, leading to greater adaptiveness. New encounters with moderately novel events in the environment reinitiate the same cycle which occurs repeatedly throughout the course of cognitive growth. The process of restoring equilibrium at a higher level of structural reorganization and greater adaptiveness is called equilibration. It is this process which accounts for stage transitions and the gradual evolution through qualitatively different ways of information processing and acquiring knowledge in Piaget's theory. He does not ignore the traditionally cited factors in development. These are experience with the physical world, heredity and neurological maturation, and social transmission. However, such factors are not sufficient in themselves and must rely upon the fourth factor of equilibration which serves as a coordinating facilitating force.

Equilibration is a self-regulating activity. The organism acting upon the environment experiences negative feedback that is incongruent with the present level of structural development. The ensuing disequilibrium motivates structural change to the point at which the novel information can be assimilated, whereby equilibrium is restored. It should be evident that this process of increasingly greater adaptiveness is not predicated upon mere conformity or adjustment. Each level of cognitive reorganization widens the scope of mental activity, frees the organism from earlier constraints, and promotes greater mastery of reality. All of this is to say that with such development occurring the individual achieves greater competence and command over himself and the environment. The values and morals that will infuse this enhanced freedom are, in large measure, the subject of this book.

Some examples of feedback inducing disequilibrium may prove instructive at this point. Illustrations are pervasive throughout the work of Piaget and others of the Geneva school. In one experiment Piaget describes the activity of an infant who pulls a support which holds a desired object toward himself. To test whether the infant truly has the scheme which promotes understanding of the relationship between object and support, the position of the object is varied. If the infant does not possess the scheme, he may still be observed pulling the support toward himself even when the object has been placed alongside the support rather than upon it. A facial expression of surprise reveals that the child had an expectation that the object would move toward him when he pulled the support. This misexpectation induces disequilibrium and leads to further grappling with the environment in order to resolve the problem and restore equilibrium. The restoration of equilibrium is predicated upon the development of a new cognitive structure which enables the infant to understand the relationship between support and object. The ineffective strategy of pulling the support when the object is alongside it will now be eliminated in favor of the effective action of pulllng it only when the object rests upon it. The new structure permits differentiation between the two states of the object in relation to the support and is clearly more adaptive. Although the state of incongruity or discrepancy between structure and experience may be viewed as one of tension, it would be a misplaced emphasis to construe the equilibrating process as having the primary goal of tension reduction. The reduction of tension is a secondary byproduct of the natural surge toward greater adaptiveness. Proponents of the Geneva school have devised a variety of ingenious experiments to induce cognitive conflict in training experiments with the aim of accelerating growth. One method is to ask the preoperational child to predict the level that liquid will attain when being poured from a short and wide beaker to a tall and thin one. The idea is that a disconfirmation of the prediction will generate surprise and lead to a resolution based upon conserving judgments. Still another method is to ask a preoperational child confronted with a set of twelve wooden beads in two different colors to place all the beads of one color on one side and all the wooden beads of the complete set on the opposite side. It is anticipated that the logical impossibility of dividing the beads this way will induce a cognitive conflict and lead the child to decenter as he is forced to differentiate between the whole and its subparts while coordinating the two perspectives simultaneously. In general, training experiments based upon this kind of strategy have met with greater success than alternate approaches. An important qualifier, however, must be inserted here. The tendency is for those subjects who already proved to be at an intermediary stage during the pretest in relation to the experimental task to exhibit the most significant gains at the time of the posttest. This is interpreted to signify that one's present level of cognitive development imposes meaning upon stimuli presented by the environment; an interpretation clearly in opposition to traditional stimulus-response learning theories. The most contemporary position emanating from the Geneva school on these training studies is to be found in a work by Inhelder, Sinclair, and Bovet, *Learning and the Development of Cognition*. Piaget has recently written a book, *The Development of Thought,* in which he offers the most thorough exposition of his equilibration theory available thus far.

## CONCLUSION

As it interacts with the environment over time from birth onward, the human organism undergoes a progression of decentrations through which the knower becomes increasingly less egocentric and more objective. Acting upon the environment he invents cognitive structures for more adaptive knowing. The practical intelligence of the sensorimotor period is interiorized as representational thought emerges. Continuing to act upon the environment, the growing child constructs complex interrelated mental action systems for processing information. The external world does not impose meaning upon the person, but through assimilation to one's developmental level and the process of autoregulation the person confers meaning upon the environment. Hence, acts of knowing involve the process of mental transformations.

# Chapter Two

# Piagetian Roots
# in Moral Judgment

Jean Piaget's fifth book, *The Moral Judgment of the Child,* was written over forty years ago. It constitutes the last of what is generally known as his early work and predates the construction of his complex logico-mathematical models. Nevertheless, although he has by now written more than fifty books and hundreds of articles, this one book alone would have assured him eminence as a pioneer in the field of sociocognitive moral development. Piaget never again devoted a major work to moral development and has given only brief treatment to it in the years following publication of this work. Yet the book has spawned a spate of replicated and modified studies, none of which have disconfirmed the essential validity of Piaget's contribution. The most ambitious of these has been the work of Lawrence Kohlberg and his collaborators, which has refined and extended Piaget's earlier work to a considerable degree. Their findings and theoretical formulations will be examined in detail later in this study, while the present chapter will focus upon the Piagetian point of departure.

Piaget's investigations on moral development emphasized the verbally communicated judgments that children from five to thirteen years of age make when stories involving a moral component are posed to them. He did not explore the relationship between those judgments and behavior, as is being done in current research. However, he does comment that children's behavior may reflect a developmental lag, so that they may be carrying out actions in the moral sphere that are more sensitively related to others than their conceptualized version of morality would suggest. The paradoxical reciprocal to this, however, is the common phenomenon in which adult individuals demonstrating an advanced moral conception fail to act upon it. Piaget himself demonstrated a precursor to this among youngsters who break the rules of marble playing while maintaining that the rules are immutable and sacred. In regard to the sequentiality of moral stages, Piaget cautions against construing this in absolute terms. There are definite age trends in which earlier and more primitive moral conceptions diminish as later and more mature ones emerge increasingly. However, there is a considerable mix of primitive and mature moral judgments which may characterize the child's thought at the same time in development. Even after the latter are clearly in greater evidence, it may be observed that they will be applied only to some areas which are of lesser complexity, and not until later will they be applied to areas of greater complexity. Piaget remarks upon this especially in reference to children's developing attitudes toward rules, a point of no minor significance since he holds that one's attitudes regarding rules constitute the essence of morality. There exists a premoral stage which is basically asocial. Following this are the two major stages of moral development in the Piagetian model. The first is a morality of constraint in which deference to external authority is the primary characteristic. It is referred to often as the stage of heteronomy and roughly corresponds to the preoperational cognitive period of development. The second is a morality of cooperation in which group solidarity and mutual respect are paramount. It is referred to as the stage of autonomy and corresponds to the period of concrete operations. Piaget's pathbreaking book is divided into four main sections. It begins with an exposition of children's attitudes toward rules and their behavior in relation to them. This is followed by a section on adult constraint and the correlated concept of moral realism. The next section explores the idea of justice and notions children have of punishment. The final portion examines the two moralities in a social context. The influences of Bovet, Baldwin, and Durkheim are cited by Piaget at various points throughout the text.

# CHANGING CONCEPTIONS AND PRACTICES
## OF THE RULES

The stories Piaget designed to test out children's responses to moral situations were based upon content familiar to them from their everyday lives. In exploring their conceptions of rules, Piaget actually got down on his hands and knees and played a familiar game with them. He selected the game of marbles because of its universality. He took the trouble to learn the intricacies of the game, although he concealed this fact from his young companions. Piaget, then, while playing the game with the children, proceeded to inquire what they thought the origin and nature of rules to be. In addition, he observed the practices they followed so that he could discover the relationship between conception and action. This is the one exception, incidentally, to the general statement that Piaget studied moral judgment only and not behavior. It is emphasized that the game of marbles is by no means a simple matter, as it permits numerous legitimate variations and this enhances its functional capacity for discovering how children relate to rules. The attitudes revealed by the participants do not signify that conceptions about rules had been carefully thought out in advance. Their attitudes do not represent preconceived ideas, but instead are the spontaneous responses to the inquiries being made. This same qualifier obtains as well to Piaget's earlier works, in which he sought to uncover the child's spontaneous thoughts about how the world is made and about the natural phenomena within it.

There are four stages observed in the child's practice of marbles. *Motoric* habits and desire dictate the manner in which the child deals with marbles in the first stage. There are no collective rules being followed, as the motor rule of this stage is purely individual and is merely ritualistic or habitual. There follows an *egocentric* stage which may begin between two to five years and extends to the age of seven years. The child during this time becomes aware of the existence of external rules governing the game and he plays in a manner attempting to initiate them. Nevertheless, the spirit of his game playing remains individualistic in that we find him either playing separately from others or, if engaged with others, he does not aim to win. The notion of winning has not yet dawned upon him. It is at about seven or eight years that the third stage emerges. Piaget refers to it as *incipient cooperation* to reflect the budding of social activity in playing the game. Although there is a lack of specificity and uniformity regarding the rules among players of this stage, each one attempts to win. The players attempt to unify the rules and may even succeed over the course of a single game, but there persists a vagueness about the rules, which are not generalized from one game to the next. A stage known as the *codification of rules* becomes manifest at about eleven or twelve. At this point the fine details of each rule and variation are carefully worked out and consensually acknowledged. The rules are universally applied across each game and locality where it is played. An earnest effort at consistent adherence to the rules is made and generally achieved. There has occurred a shift from an emphasis on cooperation to an interest in rules in their own right. This last stage coincides with the beginning of formal operations.

The second or egocentric stage is viewed as an intermediate one which comes between the purely individualistic motoric stage and the socially cooperative third stage. Although sincere in his attempt to initiate the rule, the egocentric child's activities are not at all coordinated with the game playing of other participants in the game. There is a desire to be a member of the group at play and particularly to emulate the older boys, but egocentric players do not have the capacity in the preoperational period to unify their use of rules in game playing. The essence of the following stage is the social cooperation that characterizes the game playing. Children in the third stage not only play to win, but attempt to do so while adhering to consensually agreed upon rules. The cooperative interaction demanded by playing the game this way is facilitated by the reciprocity of reversible thinking which is present in the concrete operational period. Although this aspect of development continues, the accent in the fourth stage is upon the nature of the rules themselves which, indeed, acquire a fascinating hold upon the child's mind. Piaget states, "Children of the fourth stage . . . have thoroughly mastered their code and even take pleasure in juridical discussions, whether of principle or merely of procedure, which may at times arise out of the points in dispute."[1]

There are only three stages in the development of conscious attitudes toward rules and they do not all coincide exactly with the chronological unfolding of actual practice in the game. The first stage is one in which there is no consciousness of the coercive or obligatory element in rules, despite the very young child's tendency toward engaging repetitively in a motoric scheme. At the same time, the fact is that the child has been exposed to regularities of action imposed by his environment and, thus, upon first encountering marbles, there may be some dawning awareness that rules are involved in their use. The second stage in the consciousness of rules begins at about age four or five and extends to about eight or nine, that is, to the middle of the cooperative stage in the actual practice of rules. During this period the child decisively experiences the coercive element in rules. He views rules as sacred and not subject to the possibility of change. From four to six, there is a misleading appearance of accepting a change in rules, but upon analysis it is found that the apparently accepted change had not been recognized as an innovation, but itself had been mistaken for a perennial rule. By age six even this misleading aspect has disappeared and the conception of rules as absolutely immutable is unmistakable. Although the egocentric child is found to express a belief that rules may never be changed and he even strives to imitate, he will be observed departing from rules with both minor and major infractions in practice. The rule for such a child remains external and has no binding effect upon him for this reason: the child believes that even if all children were to agree to change a rule they would be wrong to think they could succeed; so great is the reverence the child at this stage has for the sacred nature of a rule. Piaget makes the point that the egocentric child is not entirely presocial. To the extent that he is not in the cooperative stage in the practice of rules, he is presocial. However, to the extent that he embraces the rule as unchanging and external, he is not. A belief in the immutable nature of rules derives from unilateral respect, a blind acceptance of parental authority and of God, the sources of rules. There is a self-imposed quality of constraint here which nevertheless has a definite social aspect. The egocentric child moves into the cooperative stage of practicing rules while retaining a conscious attitude of their eternal nature, even though he is achieving a recognition behaviorally that the players may themselves vary the rules. There is a lag in development during this phase between the behavioral and conceptual planes; one in which the former is more advanced than the latter. The third stage in the consciousness of rules starts at about age ten, approximately the middle of the stage of cooperation in practice, and extends throughout the phase of codification. Piaget comments, "Autonomy follows upon heteronomy: the rule of a game appears to the child no longer as an external law, sacred in so far as it has been laid down by adults; but as the outcome of a free decision and worthy of respect in the measure that it has enlisted mutual consent."[2] The emphasis now is upon procedure rather than outcome. Rules may certainly be altered as long as the proper procedure gaining mutual consent is pursued. The established order is no longer revered and if it is the will of the members of a group collectively, then innovations may be explored and tested. The children now come to realize that there is no such thing as the eternal origin of rules imposed upon the game of marbles, but instead that other children, much like themselves, had gathered together around a number of marbles and generated a set of rules to facilitate playing the game. It is precisely this awakening recognition of the origin and nature of rules that leads to a spontaneous obedience in playing the game that characterizes the period of codification. Piaget emphasizes the democratic basis of this newly evolved moral achievement. Procedure and the will of the collective now govern. The children are no longer bound by a false notion of eternal and unerring tradition. An era of genuine cooperation replaces the previous period of incipient cooperation as this new consciousness of rules arises to guide codification. The rational foundation of this genuine cooperation is a more complete plane of reciprocity than any that had preceded. There must be fairness in playing the game, and therefore all participants are subject to the same laws of chance and opportunities for winning.

There is a vital point which arises here in relation to Kohlberg's writings on stage five. We will see a distinct resemblance between that stage and what has just been described from Piaget's work. Yet Kohlberg does not find such a democratic morality emerging until considerably later in development than the youngsters in Piaget's studies would suggest. Perhaps anticipating this dilemma, Piaget raises the question of such a democratic attitude arising so early when it is well known that even many adults have not arrived at that level in some domains in their life. As one would expect, Piaget's observation on the matter is somewhat ingenious. He points out that since children generally discontinue playing marbles shortly after age thirteen, if not sooner, then it follows that there are no elders for these young people to look up to as far as tradition in marbles is concerned. Those who have reached the age of twelve and thirteen are, in fact, the seniors upon whom all younger children rely as custom bearers. It is this situation which forces upon the senior youngsters a recognition of their own potential for autonomy. In the event that children customarily played the game for a much longer period, then the democratic attitude would be a longer time in developing. For Piaget, the history of the children's game of marbles is as illuminating to that population of little people as is the history of government and religion to the older population of adults.

## MORAL REALISM AND OBJECTIVE RESPONSIBILITY

The concept of realism was first introduced by Piaget in discussing the child's tendency of mind to ascribe external substantial existence to such psychic components as dreams and names. He once again utilizes the same notion in presenting his ideas pertaining to the moral realm. He succinctly formulates, "We shall therefore call moral realism the tendency which the child has to regard duty and the value attaching to it as self-subsistent and independent of the mind, as imposing regardless of the circumstances in which the individual may find himself." [3] He is explicit in citing the three criteria to which moral realism conforms. First, the good is defined by obedience to adult rule, hence moral realism is heteronomous. Second, it is the letter of the law which must be met. There is no allowance for flexibility or deviation. Third, objective responsibility determines the measure of culpability when assessing actions. It is the actual consequences of an act and not the intention motivating it which is taken into consideration.

⟨Piaget explores objective responsibility specifically with stories posed to children in the areas of clumsiness and stealing in one section and lying in another.⟩Clumsiness is accurately identified as a fairly common event in the child's life which fairly frequently evokes a negative response from adults. The stories constructed by Piaget juxtaposed one in which the damaging consequence of an act was great, while the child was either well-intentioned or merely carrying out an act precipitated by chance, to one in which only a slight damaging consequence resulted from an intentional violation of a command. An example is a story of a little boy who opens a dining room door upon being called and in so doing upsets a tray on the other side which had been resting on a nearby chair. All fifteen cups that had been supported by the tray fall and break. The alternate story is one in which a young boy left alone by his mother enters the cupboard and climbs up high to get some jam. In the process he knocks over a cup and it breaks. The clear implication is that he knows he was not to go after the jam. Upon relaying the stories, the investigator then asks whether the two children are equally guilty and, if not, which one is guiltier. The respondent must then explain why he has answered as he did. The results that Piaget obtained indicate that until age ten there will be found two types of responses among children. The same child may even alternate between the two types. One of these responses focuses exclusively on the objective damage and the other on motives. However, there is a decisive diminution of objective responsibility with age and there were no such instances of children focusing mainly on material damage rather than intention after age ten. It is Piaget's view that objective responsibility has its source in adult constraint. In relation to clumsiness, a subtle distinction is made by Piaget. The adult will often model objective responsibility, for he will scold even when the child accidentally breaks something of value, but he does not truly believe the child is morally flawed. However, the child, unlike the adult, makes no such distinction and the actor, himself or a peer, is morally at fault.

Either through repeated acts of scolding or by simply asserting prohibitions, the adult has fostered a notion of absolute obligations and forbidden behaviors. Hence, Piaget suggests that, deriving from the child's unilateral respect and the adult's constraint, moral realism is generated. In his discussion in this area, Piaget is most sensitive to the parents' potential for promoting subjective responsibility in the child by instituting certain egalitarian procedures. In addressing himself to the attempt to facilitate a responsiveness to intentions over objective damage, Piaget anticipated the work of Robert Selman by several decades. Piaget's observations are worth citing in this connection. He states, "In this way the child will find himself in the presence, not of a system of commands requiring ritualistic and external obedience, but of a system of social relations such that everyone does his best to obey the same obligations, and does so out of mutual respect."[4] It is reciprocity, in which individuals in the social system come to take the other's point of view and evaluate accordingly, that underpins the morality of this social system, and not a rigid obedience to external rule.

Piaget finds lying a particularly fertile practice around which to explore the child's developing moral conceptions because it is so integral to egocentric thought. There is a fundamental conflict inherent in lying in the face of adult constraint. Analysis of children's protocols reveals that the youngest children conceive of a lie as saying naughty words. It is the utterance of forbidden expressions. Yet the very same child is demonstrated to have an understanding that to lie is to speak what is not true. The child's extension of the definition of a lie to encompass the use of naughty words is explained by Piaget's belief that the child sees language as the means through which lying as a moral fault is committed. Saying naughty words is also to display a fault through language. The child reasons further that lies are all those things which one is not supposed to say. Although generally children between six and ten years will define a lie more simply as something that is untrue, their genuine comprehension is limited because they omit the component of intention. It is not necessarily that he cannot distinguish between intentional and unintentional statements that are untrue. The point is that for the young child, if the statement is known to be untrue, then it is held to be a lie regardless of motivation. A child who is frightened by a large dog in the street is said to be lying when he runs to his mother in alarm, announcing that he has seen a dog as big as a cow. It is at about ten or eleven years that children unambiguously recognize a lie as an intentional untruth. Surprising though it may be, Piaget discovered that younger children believed that a lie further from the truth and thus less likely to be believed was more naughty than a lie more likely to be believed because it was closer to the truth. In other words, the more successful the deception, the less naughty the liar. This proved to be the case even where the intention was not malevolent, as in the story where the boy said he saw a dog as large as a cow. Age progression leads to a reversal of this interpretation by the child and we find that older children realize that a blatant untruth is more an exaggeration than a lie. Piaget is most emphatic in conveying that he is not positing two pure stages, one sequentially followed by the other. Both objective and subjective responsibility can be found in various proportions among the younger children. The passage of time, however, leads to a significant disappearance of the former and a dominance of the latter. Gutkin, in "An Analysis of the Concept of Moral Intentionality," views the notion of intentionality as part of the broader area of personal responsibility and he offers an enriching analysis of the subject.

Truth, for the egocentric child, holds no special value. He is governed by his own desires and fantasies. Assimilation predominates over accommodation with the aim of supplying personal satisfaction. The valuing of truth evolves as the child becomes more of a social agent gradually recognizing the moral demand of reciprocity and cooperation in relationships. As long as a relation of unilateral respect is maintained the child has no opportunity to hold peer-level discussions of genuine mutual exchange and in the process to discover the destructive aspects of lying. Unilateral respect is bound to generate objective responsibility. As unilateral respect declines, the child will interiorize necessary rules and make them autonomously his own. Mutual respect replaces adult constraint and the need for truthfulness as a constructive force in relationships becomes evident. The successful lie is now seen for the invidious force that it represents. Trust must be maintained in social relations and only truthfulness can be relied upon to achieve this. It is between the ages of ten and twelve that a full consciousness of what has been discussed here becomes apparent to the child. In Piaget's words, "Thus truthfulness gradually ceases to be a duty imposed by heteronomy and becomes an object envisaged as good by an autonomous personal conscience."[5] For the very young child a lie is considered wrong because it is that which gets punished. If punishment were not a consequence of lying, then the onus of being wrong would be removed from the lie. There is a progression with age to a realization that even if lying were not something for which punishment is received, it would still be wrong in itself. However, this realization is still not accompanied by interpersonal awareness and psychological insight. It is at the next stage of development that children characterized by a high level of reciprocity awaken to the fact that lying is necessarily wrong because it is in stark opposition to maintaining mutual trust and would sunder the affective bond.

## JUSTICE AND PUNISHMENT

There are basically two types of justice, retributive and distributive. The former is concerned primarily with proportionate punishment and the latter with equality in distributing resources that are available. Piaget has observed in his studies that when the two are in conflict the younger child favors retributive action and the older child favors distributive justice. The stages of justice involve a shift from believing that whatever authority commands as punishment is just, to a conviction that a rigid equality ("a blow for a blow") is just, to a realization that equity, which takes into account a variety of factors, is the basis for justice.

Justice, in Piaget's view, is not an implant derived from external authority. The only necessary ingredients are mutual respect and solidarity among children themselves. In fact, the derivation of the justice idea in children is not only independent of adults, but is sometimes at the adult's expense.

Piaget distinguishes sharply between two kinds of punishment. Expiatory punishment is governed by constraint. A moral transgressor must be brought back into line. Punishment is coercive and proportionate to the seriousness of the violation. It is also unrelated to the content of the violation. Reciprocal punishments are not arbitrary and lack the coercive element. Hence, one who has ruptured the social bond through some transgression should simply be punished in such a way that he experiences the natural consequences of that rupture. In order of severity, punishment by reciprocity has been classified as follows: 1) exclusion from the group, permanently or temporarily; 2) being subjected to the transgression's immediate and material consequences; 3) deprivation of whatever it is that has been misused; 4) performing upon the child the exact violation he has committed; 5) restitution, in which the offender must replace or repay for what is damaged; 6) censure, which entails no punishment other than communicating to the transgressor that he has, indeed, broken the bond of solidarity. In general, nonexpiatory punishment ultimately seeks the restoration of solidarity and not mere conformity. There is an age trend leading away from expiation toward reciprocity in punishment. Kohlberg states the following in connection with Piaget's studies:

Four-year-old children do not use reciprocity as a reason for consideration of others, whereas children of seven and older frequently do. Even seven-year-olds show mainly selfish and concrete reciprocity concerns, including anticipation of retaliation and anticipation of return of favors. Most ten-year-olds who were asked, "What would the Golden Rule say to do if a boy came up and hit you?" interpreted the golden rule in terms of concrete reciprocity and said, "Hit him back. Do unto others as they do unto you." By age eleven to thirteen most children can clearly judge in terms of ideal reciprocity, in terms of putting oneself in the place of someone in a different position, and in terms of sentiments for past affection and favors.[6]

Stark reciprocity in which the governing rule is to seek an exactly proportionate response to the offense is the stage of equality which on the average is from seven to ten years of age. It can have an almost brutal effect and it is not until beyond age ten that the more just form of reciprocity, equity, predominates over equality. Further comments on the nature of equity will follow shortly.

Punishment by expiation is clearly linked to a morality of heteronomy in which pure duty and obedience reign. The ultimate source of punishment is authority with which the child lacks a relationship of reciprocity, which is not possible in an nonequalitarian relationship. It is the morality of autonomy, grounded in mutual respect, which gives rise to a punishment ethos of reciprocity. Expiative punishment has roots in primitive vengeance, whereas reciprocity evolves from it and through strict equality to a morality of forgiveness and understanding. The essence of punishment by reciprocity in its most evolved form is, for Piaget, inducing an awareness in the transgressor that he has broken the bond of solidarity.

Piaget points out that there may exist a conflict between retributive and distributive justice. For example, if a very young child drops a roll while hiking with a group in the mountains and the roll irretrievably falls over the side, should he be given another? Younger children responding to such a dilemma would choose a retributive response, stating that he was wrong to let it fall over the side and should not be given more. As children grow older, they favor distributive justice, indicating that it would be unfair not to redistribute what remains in order that the young child might have a part of what is still available. As children first begin favoring distributive justice, they will explain their position simply by stating that all should have equal shares. As they move beyond sheer equality to equity they will support their responses by introducing relevant variables, suggesting that the child is too young, for example, to understand and could not be held responsible for what happened. Equity is situational in the sense that the specific conditions obtaining are taken into account and coordinated to arrive at a just resolution. This is a more subtle and complex advance over advocating pure equality in either distributive or retributive spheres. In commenting upon the shift from authority-based concepts of justice to equalitarian justice, Piaget comments, "Equalitarian justice develops with age at the expense of submission to adult authority, and in correlation with solidarity between children. Equalitarianism would therefore seem to come from habits of reciprocity peculiar to mutual respect rather than from the mechanisms of duties that is founded upon unilateral respect."[7] Equity, in Piaget's view, extends equalitarianism one step further than the pure equality which defines it, to encompass the relative aspects of a given situation. In summary, Piaget posits three major periods in the child's developing conception of justice. In the first period justice is subordinated to the authority of adults. This generally lasts until seven or eight years. Ranging from ages eight to eleven, the child's sense of justice is observed becoming increasingly more equalitarian. Finally there emerges the third major period at about eleven or twelve at which time equalitarianism yields to the relativity of equity.

Finally, there is a curious tendency of the young mind to adhere to what Piaget calls immanent justice. The child expects that wrongdoing will automatically bring with it a corolary punishment. It is in the nature of things that this will occur. Perhaps it is not really a surprising belief if one considers that there is no pure chance operative in the world of the preoperational child. That world is infused with purposiveness and finalism. Although immanent justice extends into the school years, it diminishes with age and is finally abandoned.

## DURKHEIM, BOVET, AND BALDWIN

The closing section of Piaget's work on the child's moral development expands into the field of sociology and social psychology. Three influential theorists, Durkheim, Bovet, and Baldwin are treated at length by Piaget.

Durkheim was a French sociologist who formulated a theory of morality whose ultimate source was society and whose major aim was conformity to society's rules. Piaget stresses that a failing in Durkheim's view is to ignore the fact that children have a society of peers available to them and, hence, are not exclusively subject to adult authority. An autonomous morality cannot be truly transmitted by a teacher or any authority, although Durkheim thought it could be. It must be constructed by each individual through interaction with peers, and by those adults who relate to the child with equality, in mutual respect. Piaget's formulations lead him to advocate the creation of a democratic society within the school system and to stress the student's own initiative. He somewhat sharply refers to the type of school that Durkheim advocates as being a monarchy acquiring its authority from divine right.

Bovet holds that a sense of obligation arises from being issued commands by those whom one respects. There is nothing intrinsic to the law itself to which the mind yields. A difficulty inherent in Bovet's formulation is that since assent is compelled by unilateral respect, the rule promulgated by an authority may or may not be intrinscially good. Piaget points out that the emphasis on respect, however, allows for a shift from unilateral to mutual respect. The transition to mutuality, as a qualitatively different stage, which Piaget emphasizes, eliminates coercion and invokes reciprocity, assuring the formation of rational rules subject to mutual regulation.

Baldwin elaborates upon the point that at birth there exists no sense of self whatever and it is only by interacting with other individuals and especially by imitation that it can be acquired. There is generated in the process an "ideal self," which is in a sense an internalized command, imitating the authority from whence it sprung, that serves to convey what one ought to become. An inner sense of the morality of law and the good evolves to a point where it is seen as superior to individuals, beyond the dictates of authority figures, and ultimately elevated to a stage of absolute moral law.

Piaget does not believe that Baldwin, even though he posits an adualism between inner consciousness and outer reality, sufficiently appreciates the child's egocentrism. The child's egocentrism specifically places his own viewpoint at an absolute position. Hence, although the child appears to respect commands, his egocentrism leads to distortion and misapplication of them. Piaget insists that while imitation will illuminate for us what we have in common with others, it does not promote a particularized self. In an illuminating passage he states the following:

> In order to discover oneself as a particular individual, what is needed is a continuous comparison, the outcome of opposition, of discussion, and of mutual control; and indeed consciousness of the individual self appears

far later than consciousness of the more general features in our psychological make-up. This is why a child can remain egocentric for a very long time (through lack of consciousness of self), while participating on all points in the minds of others. It is only by knowing our individual nature with its limitations as well as its resources that we grow capable of coming out of ourselves and collaborating with other individual natures. Consciousness of self is therefore both a product and a condition of cooperation.[8]

The work of Baldwin has held significance for both Piaget and Kohlberg. Kohlberg, in "Stage and Sequence," decries the relative neglect of Baldwin's work by researchers today and has offered a rather extensive treatment of his theories. It is worth noting, in passing, that although Piaget is justifiably credited with having created the new interdisciplinary science of genetic epistemology, the genetic psychology of Baldwin stands as an unquestioned precursor to that growing body of knowledge.

## SUMMARY OF PIAGET-BASED RESEARCH

A voluminous amount of replication research has flowed from Piaget's pioneering work, *The Moral Judgment of the Child.* A good deal of it is sector research in the sense of being designed to test a specific hypothesis such as one involving objective responsibility versus intentional judgment. On the other hand, some of it is addressed to broader issues such as the universality of stage sequences. An exhaustive survey will not be attempted, but instead I shall identify the major findings that previously conducted surveys have revealed to date.

Kohlberg cites eleven areas in which age changes are said to occur in Piaget's moral developmental theory.[9] He divides these into two groups; those areas in which age trends have been confirmed and those in which they have not been. The six dimensions supported by the research at the time of Kohlberg's survey are as follows: 1) intentionality judgments ascend in frequency over time as objective responsibility declines; 2) older children show a greater recognition that different perspectives may be adopted regarding the same situation, whereas younger children center on only one perspective as the right one; 3) independence of sanctions. For an older child a bad act is so because of its intrinsic nature, but a younger child will construe an act as bad solely on the basis of someone being punished for performing it; 4) there is an increase in the use of reciprocity from four through thirteen years, as predicted by Piaget; 5) the administration of harsh punishment during the younger years, with a gradual diminution of such practices, is advocated, as well as an ascending frequency with age in favor of restitution and reform; 6) there is a tendency on the part of younger children to think that harmful events will automatically and naturally follow bad actions, but older children do not anticipate such teleological events.

Age trends in the above area have been supported by the research, at least in Western cultures. These developmental trends have been observed to occur irrespective of religion, social class, and story content when being questioned. Child rearing practices regarding punishment may vary without eliminating the observed early characteristics in young children of absolutism, objective responsibility, and orientation to punishment. Kohlberg suggests that the cultural variations are not causal to these features of moral development, but that some of them may lead to deceleration or stage arrest. The cognitive developmental basis of moral development is indicated in the positive correlation found between the areas confirmed and I.Q. scores. Lastly, each of the six aspects demonstrates a fundamental shift in orientation from emphasizing objective material consequences to subjective psychological components.

Kohlberg reports that the areas of Piagetian research which have been disconfirmed are not those with cognitive bases, but those that are rooted in what he calls socioemotional elements. In these areas, he asserts, there may be found an increase with age of the anticipated developments followed by a decline in their presence. A clear-cut emergence of a democratic spirit preceded by an authoritarian ethic is not observed. Kohlberg also concludes that the research does not support the premise that peer interaction among young children promotes either reciprocity or intentionality, even though he acknowledges that it plays a significant role in general moral development. He does contend, however, that social participation among preadolescents will facilitate the acquisition of more mature moral conceptions with respect to his own posited stages of development. The shift from unilateral to mutual respect is not fully supported and, in any event, we will see that Kohlberg places a different interpretation upon the nonegalitarian relationship between child and adult than does Piaget. There is greater variance to be found in these areas of socioemotional aspects as influenced by religion, social class and culture, and content of stories utilized. This is in marked contrast to those dimensions with a cognitive foundation, which are resistant to these variables. Lickona, in what appears to be the most current survey available on Piaget-based research, has reached a conclusion similar to Kohlberg's. He states the following:

> The findings . . . . suggest that while Piaget's analysis of the cognitive basis of moral judgment is well formed, his speculations about its affective side are on shaky grounds. Young children do not . . . stand in awe of the authority of adults or the rules they repeatedly set forth. . . . The research . . . indicates that loyalty to and genuine respect for personal authority, like respect for rules, is something that children must *develop* during the early school years (ages 4–7) and something that accompanies *advance,* not immaturity, on moral dimensions such as judging the rightness of an action apart from its external consequences. The child's early obedience orientation in moral thinking appears to be based less on respect for the moral status of adults than on simple recognition of their superior power.[10]

In view of its extreme relevance to the subject at hand, it will be fruitful to examine Lickona's report at greater length. He is emphatic in asserting that the evidence is ample to unequivocally accept Piaget's position of developmental changes in the area of moral judgments, reflecting qualitatively different moral modes of thought that change with age and experience. Nevertheless, the data pertaining to specific areas is mixed, some of it lending support and some not doing so. As with all research, it should be kept in mind that disconfirming evidence may at times be explained by flawed conceptual analysis or methodology. Even so, when faced with such deficiencies in a given piece of research, the most one can conclude is "Not proven". Lickona, in an article, "Piaget Misunderstood," that predates the research survey presently under consideration, has provided an excellent critique of misconceptions about Piaget's theory of moral development, which have led to false or irrelevant conclusions in the research literature.

A major disclosure is that moral developmental advances appear at a much slower rate than originally proposed. We are more likely to find youngsters achieving Piaget's morality of autonomy between the ages of twelve to seventeen rather than at age twelve. Furthermore, Piaget's highest stage of autonomy would seem to be coincident with Kohlberg's third stage, signifying three additional major steps which one could possibly pass through. Clearly, the autonomous morality uncovered in the prototypical study by Piaget will be seen to fall far short of the highest level of moral reasoning on the Kohlbergian scale, to be explored in chapter 4 of this volume.

With only minor deviation, all of the six areas Kohlberg reported as being confirmed by the literature were reaffirmed by Lickona's assessment of Piagetian replication and modified studies.

In general, although it is not the only significant variable, there is a positive correlation between mental age and Piagetian moral development. However, an individual's I.Q. does not reflect intellectual level in the manner that Piaget, himself, has conceived of it. Therefore, it is noteworthy that Lickona is able to cite several projects validating a positive correlation between moral judgment measures of the Piagetian variety and competence at performing Piagetian tasks of a logical nature. These findings lend support to the cognitive foundation of moral development. A detailed study of the connection between cognitive level of development and the Kohlbergian stages of morality will appear in a later chapter.

Lickona has further inquired into the role of both peer interaction and absence of adult constraint to ascertain their impact upon progress toward a morality of cooperation. In a summary statement, Lickona reflects on the following:

> For all three hypothesized causes of moral change—cognitive development, experience of social equality, and increased independence of adult constraint—the research reviewed thus far has been correlational rather than experimental. The most that can be said on the basis of these naturalistic data is that the factors identified by Piaget as sources of moral growth have typically been found to correlate with mature judgment on one or another of his dimensions. The evidence is strongest for the role of cognitive development, mixed but generally supportive regarding the contribution of peer experience, and weakest with respect to the role of freedom from the constraining influence of adult authority.[11]

Lickona goes on to review experimental studies designed to foster moral growth in Piagetian areas. His overall conclusion is that it does not appear plausible to expect accelerated growth from the types of causes involved, such as cognitive development and peer interaction, in so short a period of time as a laboratory experiment utilizes. He concludes with a recommendation of longitudinal studies with careful follow-up as the most appropriate approach to experimental research of a developmental theory.

Hoffman, in "Moral Development," has presented a balanced and evenhanded discourse ranging widely across many approaches to moral development. Attention here will focus upon his comments on consistency across moral attributes in Piagetian theory. The purpose in concentrating on these remarks is not to cite definitive conclusions, but to highlight some issues involved when dealing with Piaget's complex moral system. Hoffman begins with the premise that it is reasonable, given the nature of cognitive developmental theory, to expect to find considerable consistency across attributes. One may search for consistency of a single attribute across different content areas. He cites the example of objective responsibility being applied to the two spheres of lying and stealing. There is also a type of consistency which deals with the interrelatedness of two distinct attributes. For example, one may search for a correlation in development between objective responsibility and immanent justice, both early modes of moral judgment in Piaget's theory. Hoffman concluded from a review of the literature that despite some mixed findings, in general, the evidence did not support a view of stages as structured wholes which consistently cut across all areas. It is his conceptual analysis of this conclusion that I am interested in pinpointing.

Peer-level experience is an important facilitator of moral development in Piaget's view, but it obviously does not occur at the same time in children's lives in all areas. Specifically, social interaction with peers in the game of marbles may very well promote autonomous attitudes toward rules in this area, yet the children may, for the time being, remain heteronomous in relation to rules applied to other areas in their lives. Piaget himself made the identical point in his book on the subject. Similarly, intentional judgments may emerge in situations entailing behavior resulting in physical damage before it is observed in situations involving lying, since the latter is less palpable and more subtle. In other words, research must take into account décalages in development, a phenomenon which is integral to a cognitive structural approach and does not run counter to it.

Another consideration is that of the complexity of situation and variables. As the child's cognitive capacities increase, he is more likely to take into account additional variables, especially more complex ones. Hoffman suggests that while it is an advance, making a judgment based on intentions over physical consequences when inanimate objects are involved is relatively simple in comparison to continuing to hold a well-intentioned person responsible for harm his actions have caused another person, when the unfavorable consequences could have been anticipated and, hence, avoided. In the case of the latter judgment, good intentions are recognized and yet the actor is not absolved from responsibility for his behavior.

Hoffman's observation is that research designed to test out consistency across stages in Piagetian moral theory has not instituted the proper controls needed to take into account the complexity of the system. It is through continual rigorous conceptual and methodological analysis such as Hoffman has demonstrated that progress in researching all facets of cognitive developmental psychology will occur. As for the absence of stage consistency confirmation in Piagetian moral theory specifically, a different picture will be presented in the modified and expanded work of Lawrence Kohlberg.

# Chapter Three

# Egocentrism and Social Perspectivism

[As long as the child remains embedded in his own perspective, he will be unable to progress in his capacity for moral reasoning.] The very young child is not aware that others possess a point of view which may be different from his own. Hence, in his interpersonal relations, he acts as if peers and adults share his limited outlook. He has no basis for even attempting to anticipate the needs, feelings, and motives of others. The concept of egocentrism, which represents this condition, is a rich and central one in the field of cognitive-developmental psychology. It essentially signifies an incapacity for differentiating between internal and external. In its profoundest form the epistemic subject experiences a state in which knower and known are fused together as one. All of cognitive development may be seen as a series of progressions in which there is continual disengagement between subject and object, leading to increased objectivity. However, objectivity is characterized by a relativism which takes into account the many perspectives that must be coordinated to provide knowledge of reality in a situation. Inhelder and Piaget characterize it in the following manner:

> Essentially, the process, which at any one of the developmental stages moves from egocentrism toward decentering, constantly subjects increases in knowledge to a refocusing of perspective. . . . Objectivity presupposes a decentering—i.e., a continual refocusing of perspective. Egocentrism, on the other hand, is the undifferentiated state prior to multiple perspectives, whereas objectivity implies both differentiation and coordination of the points of view which have been differentiated.[1]

The term egocentrism as it is used by the Geneva school is applied to logical, ontological, and social realms. Although there are notable exceptions, the bulk of Piaget's work utilizes it in relation to the child's construction of knowledge about the physical world. The meaning of the word in this discussion, however, will be restricted to its significance in a social context. This is in keeping with Piaget's use of the concept in his book on the language and thought of the child and the one on moral judgment, as well as his treatment of adolescence in the final chapter of his work on that developmental period. The egocentric child, then, will be viewed simply as one who centers upon his own point of view and is unaware that others hold a viewpoint of their own. Decentration refers to the ability to see things from perspectives other than one's own. It may be either sequential, in which case one shifts through time from his own to another's viewpoint, or it may be simultaneous, in which case one's own perspective and another's are coordinated at the same time. The ability to see things from another person's perspective is called role-taking. Both Piaget and Kohlberg consider role-taking to be a pivotal concept in their respective theories of moral development. It serves as a connecting or intermediary link between the necessary cognitive-structural development and the attainment of moral maturity. Because of its essential function and integral relationship to contemporary moral stage theory role-taking, or perspectivism, as it is alternately called, will be examined in depth. The leading figures in this field are Piaget, Feffer, Flavell, and Selman. The theorist who coined the term role-taking and is the forerunner of much of the work in the area, Mead, warrants attention in his own right. As the discussion proceeds it will be observed that an examination of role-taking may emphasize either the individual, an interpersonal framework, or a societal perspective. In any case, egocentrism and perspectivism are complex concepts which develop in inverse proportion. As egocentrism declines, perspectivism increases. The concepts are subject to influence by such variables as familiarity of situation, task complexity, and social class. The nature of both at varying levels of cognitive development is qualitatively different from its expression in preceding stages. Some contemporary research on the subject has been criticized for testing role-taking with tasks that invoke cognitive skills that are unrelated to role-taking itself. The problem is that the subject may actually have the ability to deal with perspectivism at some level, but the fact will be masked if the child lacks the contingent cognitive skill, which is not really essential to the main hypothesis. A false negative will then result. The corolary is that the age at which role-taking is then said to first appear is set higher than is truly the case.

## KOHLBERG'S PERSPECTIVE ON ROLE-TAKING

Since it is primarily because of the strong emphasis placed upon role-taking by Kohlberg in his moral stage theory that this material is being introduced, it may be useful to highlight the essential features of his use of the term, which he adopted from Mead. Kohlberg is quite explicit in citing the following characteristics of role-taking:

1. It emphasizes the cognitive as well as the affective side.
2. It involves an organized structural relationship between self and others.
3. It emphasizes that the process involves understanding and relating to all the roles in the society of which one is a part.
4. It emphasizes that role-taking goes on in *all* social interactions and communication situations, not merely in ones that arouse emotions of sympathy or empathy.[2]

Kohlberg is insistent that the emotional aspect of role-taking, with its implication of empathy and sympathy not be emphasized exclusively. The dual emphasis by Kohlberg is, of course, quite consistent with Piaget's position, promulgated many years earlier, on the indissociable nature of affect and cognition. There exists no pure cognition without affect, just as affect cannot arise in a vacuum without being chanelled by cognitive structuration. The structural base of affect and cognition is a shared one and, for both Piaget and Kohlberg, neither component of mental life solely determines the other. The purest act of cognition relies upon interest from the affective side to energize it. An emotion generated from within the moral sphere will derive its meaning to the individual from the sociocognitive stage of moral development that he is at. For example, anxiety precipitated by the transgression of a moral precept will be experienced very differently on a symbolic plane by the Stage 1 person than by the Stage 4 person. The meaning conferred upon the anxiety has its source in the sociocognitive moral stage from which it arose. According to

Kohlberg, the Stage 1 person may be anxious in relation to the possibility of going to jail or suffering some bad consequence to himself, whereas this would be preempted for the Stage 4 person by a sense of guilt over having broken the law, which he felt obliged to preserve.

Kohlberg, in "Stage and Sequence," presents his views on role-taking in a lengthy tract in which he formulates the cognitive-developmental position on socialization. His theoretical predecessors in this regard are Baldwin, Mead, and Piaget. He is also the intellectual heir of Kant and Dewey, whose influences will be commented upon in the next chapter.

Role-taking capacity enables one to respond to his own behavior as seen through the eyes of another, as well as to react to the other person as if he were like one's self. This is a reciprocal activity that structures the thinking and behavior of the subject. The social matrix is comprised of a number of selves that are like the own self of the subject, but are not identical with that self. The essence of a moral conflict pivots around competing and oppositional claims among two or more selves, and the key to a just resolution resides in the moral agent's role-taking ability which will be variously invoked, depending upon his stage of development. Commenting that role-taking has a wide field of applicability beyond the moral sphere, Kohlberg goes on to state, "Basically, however, all these forms imply a common structure of equality and reciprocity between selves with expectations about one another. Our moral stages represent successive forms of reciprocity, each more differentiated and universalized than the preceeding form."[3]

Since role-taking competence evolves progressively through an ongoing structuration process of increasing differentiation and integration, Kohlberg is especially concerned with social institutions that promote role-taking opportunities. It is the direct participation in the life of a group or institution that affords the growing child an opportunity for development and enhancement of role-taking. Leadership roles in particular call upon role-taking skills as decision making requires taking the roles of those who will be affected by the leader's actions. This is especially true of democratic leadership. Similarly, the nonleaders in a democratic group or institution will have greater opportunities for developing their role-taking skills, for they will be called upon to engage in the decision making process. Clearly, the first group a child belongs to is the family. Although a good family offers role-taking opportunities and a bad family, in Kohlbergian terms, may foster moral arrest and pathology, children who have not grown up in a traditional family matrix at all may still reach moral maturity. Kohlberg contrasts children from an orphanage to children raised in a kibbutz. Interaction with family members is far lesser than ordinarily for the kibbutz child and, of course, the child in the orphanage will have no parents. While the institutionalized child is found to be morally behind in development, the kibbutz child is on a par with the child raised in an urban family, from a moral standpoint. What Kohlberg is seeking to establish is that it is the role-taking opportunities which are critical to moral development in child rearing and these may be lacking in certain families on the one hand, while on the other they may be present in the environment of some children reared outside the family unit. Although one would not expect the child to be a leader in his family, the parents of a family high in role-taking activities are those who invite the child to participate in decisions, permit him to assume responsibility, encourage discussion, and point out to him his part in his own actions which affect other people, as well as his actions' consequences to them.

Peer group interaction is another major avenue providing role-taking opportunities for children. Kohlberg, like Piaget, stresses the importance of this social activity for general moral development, but he denies that it promotes growth in specific Piagetian identified moral dimensions, such as intentionality in making judgments.

Kohlberg takes a position which is in opposition to a prevailing notion in traditional sociology. The convention has been to see the growing child as beset by conflicting moral values derived from multiple commitments to family, peer group, and the broader societal institutions on a politico-economic level. Each sphere is said to generate its own values, which then place the growing young person in a quandary because of the conflict among them. Kohlberg's theory leads to a different formulation. He states, "Instead of participation in various groups causing conflicting developmental trends in morality, it appears that participation in various groups converges in stimulating the development of basic moral values, which are not transmitted by one particular group to another. . . . While various people and groups make conflicting *immediate demands* upon the child, they do not seem to present the child with basically conflicting or different stimulation for *general moral* development."[4] It is precisely because

Kohlberg's theory is founded upon a structuralist base that he may logically and consistently adopt this viewpoint. There evolves a meaningful pattern of organization through the development of moral role-taking structures which may be brought to bear in the resolution of conflict amid competing claims within any social system, regardless of its scale.

The roots of role-taking are to be found in early imitative behavior which serves a major function in the socialization process, according to Kohlberg. He cites both Baldwin and Piaget as early theorists addressing imitation in the sociocognitive development of the human organism. Imitation is not only a source of social knowledge, in that it is a reconstruction by the child of what others are observed to be doing, but in Baldwin's view it helps the child to build both a self-concept and a concept of others. Imitation is followed by a process of "ejection," in which the child ascribes to the other the feelings he himself has experienced upon imitating the other. The new activity taken on by the imitating child modifies his self-concept, as one competent to perform the action involved, and at the same time provides him with a phenomenological basis for inferring something about the other's subjective state when the other is carrying out the action. Thus, Kohlberg emphasizes that social knowledge and knowledge of the self are constructed from acts of sharing, by taking another's perspective. The development of a self is a social act motivated by a thrust toward competence. When the child at first imitates the observed behavior of the adult, he is submissive in that he is merely copying the valued action of another. However, when he initiates such action subsequently, he is seeking to reverse the roles. He is manifesting a bid for status as having moved toward the competence and mastery of the model and he intends that the model will now accord him the admiration that he had previously accorded the model. This role reversal activity appears as early as the second year. It continues as the child at three and four years of age, having imitated a model, can be seen assuming the role of being a model for others as he exhibits his budding competence in performing the activity.

Having traced the origin of role-taking behavior to imitation in early childhood, a view Kohlberg derives primarily from Baldwin, we will proceed to an examination of related work by other major theorists, some of whom have had a significant influence on Kohlberg.

## THE SYMBOLIC-INTERACTION
## THEORY OF MEAD

George H. Mead (1862–1931) was a social psychologist who adopted an interactional perspective, stressing that mind develops as a result of the organism interacting with its environment. He held that evolutionary direction could be altered by the exercise of the intellect of human beings. He wedded his social psychology to philosophy and shares a place alongside of James and Dewey as one of the great American pragmatists. Mind and consciousness are developed through a social process in which each growing individual participates. Mead believed himself to be a social behaviorist. Although he held that the starting point of theorizing should be observed behavior, he was perfectly willing to construct a theory to explain complex behavior that is not itself observable, relying as it does upon inner experience.[5] Mead's frame of reference is distinctly related to role-taking. He emphasizes that through social activity a person develops the capacity to take the role of another and in so doing observe himself symbolically as he would be seen by others. In this manner he can shift from being a subject who observes others to being an object observed by another. Out of the process of social interaction we develop a notion of a generalized other which is a composite of how we think others view and respond to us. In reflecting upon the generalized other we will sometimes modify our own anticipated behavior on the basis of how we think others may respond to us. The generalized other is molded out of many experiences in which we have taken note of how people actually have reacted to us.

In "Social Consciousness," Mead takes as the unit of analysis the specific interaction between two people in a social matrix. In an illuminating comparison he juxtaposes a man running through the forest to a man who is directly confronted with a number of combatants. The running man perceives the environment, its contours and obstacles, and will respond by adjusting his own behavior in an adaptive manner. He does not expect his adjusted movements, however, to exert a modifying force upon the environment. In the social situation the reality is different. One's own responses to the encountered stimuli can shape the course of things to come. The man who recognizes a stimulus from another which signifies he is about to be attacked may avert the attack by altering his own behavior. In observing an assaultive approach from an enemy, a man may place himself in the shoes of the other to see that if he acts boldly the enemy will back down, whereas if he assumes a submissive position, the attack will most certainly be carried out. Taking the role of the other then influences his own behavior, which in turn becomes a stimulus that modifies the intended behavior of the attacker. The man asserts himself boldly and his enemy turns to run. The course of events in a social reality has been shaped by role-taking. I have elaborated upon this illustration slightly beyond the original in order to fully capture Mead's meaning.

Although it is out of a number of specific experiences that the generalized other is forged, it takes on a transcendent character reflective of the generalized attitudes inherent in the group or community within which one holds membership. Just as in a specific situation a person may respond to the other's anticipated actions to his intended behavior, he may also respond to the anticipated reactions of the community, in the form of his generalized other, to his intended behavior. There occurs a symbolic conversation or communication within himself which, for Mead, is the thinking process. Through this symbolic activity it becomes possible for humans to engage in rational behavior. This is quite different from the limited concrete activity of animals. A dog will respond automatically and inevitably with a hostile gesture to an aggressive act from another. His response then becomes the stimulus which elicits an automatic reaction from the aggressor. Mead's point in his illustration of the animal fight is that neither can take the role of the other to anticipate either what the other will do next or how the other might respond to his own intended behavior. The fight unfolds in a linear fashion without benefit of symbolic activity which might have altered the possible course of the action and, thereby, modifying the outcome.

## PIAGET AND PERSPECTIVISM

Two major foci of Piaget's work which are of concern here are visual perspective taking and communication. Piaget and Inhelder, in *The Child's Conception of Space,* have made some interesting discoveries regarding the growing young child's capacity to literally see things from another's point of view. In a classic experiment they place a configuration of three three-dimensional simulated cardboard mountains on a table. A doll is rotated by the experimenter from one position to another. The child has ten photographs before him and his task is to select the one showing the scene the doll would see from its perspective. In a variation of the task, the child is to place the doll at a position which would give it a view corresponding to a particular picture. Lastly, he is given a set of flat cardboard pieces which he is to reconstruct to show what would appear on a snapshot if the doll were to take a picture from a specific viewpoint. The child is permitted to walk around the table, after which he is to return to his seat. The youngest children did not understand the assignment. Once the child does understand the task, however, he exhibits a totally uniperspective stance. In effect, he indicates that he thinks the scenes observed by the doll are identical with his own. It does not appear merely to be a matter of not having the ability to recreate what the other is viewing. Rather, the evidence indicates that the child simply has no awareness that the doll has a viewpoint other than the child's own. This egocentric stage lasts from four to seven years of age. Between seven and eight years the child becomes aware that there is a point of view other than his own, but his version regarding the doll's perspective at various positions is incorrect. Finally, the child at nine or ten years can also formulate the correct version, indicating that he can take the other's visual role and accurately coordinate perspectives. A variety of experiments of this type have been conducted by subsequent researchers. Some of them have involved more complex arrangements and others more simple ones. The variable of task complexity does seem to have an effect on the results. Thus we find that children perform better at a younger age when the task is more simple, but when the demands of the task are more stringent, the age for successful coordination of perspectives is pushed upward. It should not be overlooked that this experiment involves both egocentrism and cognitive skills bearing on spatial relations, which is a confounding factor.

In *The Language and Thought of the Child,* Piaget studied the process of verbal communication very early in his career. In fact, he devoted this, his first book, to this subject. Language as it exists among humans is undoubtedly one of our most fascinating and cherished attributes. Yet its first appearance in the second year of life is of limited scope as it continues to manifest its sensorimotor roots. It remains so action-laden in the beginning that many children in the early acquisition phase can actually be observed carrying out the action when using a verb. Hence, a toddler saying "jump" may be seen jumping as he speaks the word. Early language is also largely lacking in public meaning as words often carry private meanings, perhaps shared only with the mother. There occurs a diminution of these features of language as the sensorimotor imprint disappears and words become increasingly public in that they accommodate a consensual meaning. Yet there persists a serious deficiency in the child's communication pattern up to the age of six or seven. In brief, the child's speech until that time tends to be egocentric and it is not until about seven years of age that his speech shifts from egocentric to sociocentric.

Piaget's procedure was that of conducting naturalistic studies of children's spontaneous utterances, which he recorded and analyzed. The first portion of this work involved only two children, six years old, who were observed for one month. There followed a further study with twenty children between the ages of four and seven. The essential theme of *The Language and Thought of the Child* is that the child's language is limited by and an expression of his cognitive level of development. Hence, the preoperational child's language is egocentric in that he centers on his own viewpoint and makes no attempt to take the viewpoint of his listener. Therefore, his speech is not constructed to demonstrate the validity of his statements or to compel assent to them. Thoughts that are not logically related are juxtaposed without explanation. Causal connectives such as "therefore" and "because" are omitted. The referents to pronouns are omitted, leaving the listener uninformed about who "he," "she," "they," and "them" are. It is as if the child were speaking only to himself and did not realize that the listener had certain informational needs which must be conformed to if genuine communication was to take place. Piaget concluded from his study that, in fact, egocentric speech does not truly have the aim of communication. There are three subclasses of egocentric speech. There is repetition, which has nothing more than the intrinsic pleasure of talking as its aim. It bears the stamp of babbling and is not at all social. A second class is monologue, which addresses no one. The child talks aloud in a manner suggesting that he is simply speaking his thoughts. It, too, has no social function. The third type is the collective monologue. This form of egocentric speech has a quasi-social character to it, but remains noncommunicative speech. The child speaks aloud in the presence of others. He is still centered on his own actions and thoughts. At best, he seeks to draw the interest of others to himself. Although aware of the audience he is not really addressing it. The situation is compounded by the fact that peer level listeners at this stage are equally egocentric. Therefore, they are equally centered upon themselves and the observer may witness a scene of preoperational children soliloquizing amid one another without any dialogue occurring. Also, the listener who appears to be paying attention is more than likely assimilating what he hears to his own viewpoint without attempting to accommodate what is novel to him in the message. The result is that he believes he has understood when he has not. In the process of interpreting the message he has distorted it. Of course, the message was never a genuine communication in the first place.

Adaptive or sociocentric communication appears between the ages of seven and eight. It is not that children talking to one another suddenly understand everything they say to each other. However, at this time there is manifest a serious attempt to communicate effectively to one another. Children by this time have decentered from their uniperspective and take the point of view of the other while attempting to transmit information. The emphasis that Piaget has placed on peer interaction throughout his professional career has been evident from the time of his first book-length work. He states succinctly:

> What then gives rise to the need for verification? Surely it must be the shock of our thought coming into contact with that of others, which produces doubt and the desire to prove. . . . We are constantly hatching an enormous number of false ideas, conceits, utopias, mystical explanations, suspicions and megalomaniacal fantasies, which disappear when brought into contact with other people. The social need to share the thought of others and to communicate our own with success is the root of our need for verification. Proof is the outcome of argument.[6]

The conquest of egocentrism during the preoperational period and the increasing competence to take the role of another are largely the outcome of dialectical confrontation in the social arena.

The egocentrism of adolescence, manifesting itself as the youngster first enters the formal operational period, has been introduced in the opening chapter. The young person is capable now of thinking about his own thought. His own thought, therefore, may be an object of his thinking process, which is no longer confined to known objects from the environment, as in the concrete operational period. Similarly, the thoughts of other people also become the object of his newly expanded thinking prowess. However, he does not properly distinguish between what has become the primary object of his concern and what is of focal interest to others. For the adolescent, both his own and the interests of others are channeled toward himself. He labors under the false impression that his actions and appearance are of paramount concern to others. This formulation has led David Elkind, elaborating upon Piaget, to the following assertion:

> One consequence of adolescent egocentrism is that, in actual or impending social situations, the young person anticipates the reactions of other people to himself. These anticipations, however, are based on the premise that others are as admiring or as critical of him as he is of himself. In a sense, then, the adolescent is continually constructing, or reacting to, *an imaginary audience*.[7]

Elkind invokes this notion to explain much of the exaggerated and narcissistic behaviors of the adolescent and regards it as an hypothesis which gradually yields to repeated encounters with reality. This facilitates a differentiation in the adolescent's mind between his own primary interests and those of others, which he eventually comes to realize do not coincide. Thus, in early adolescence we have the paradoxical situation in which the young person is role-taking, but because of the particular form that egocentrism takes at this time, his inference leads to the construction of a highly distorted perspective which he attributes to the other.

## FEFFER'S ROLE-TAKING PARADIGM

Melvin Feffer has sought to concentrate upon expanding the social implications inherent in Piaget's fertile concept of decentration. The infant gradually decentrates from his solipsistic union with the objects in his environment. The preoperational child progressively differentiates between his own psychic properties and natural objects. He also decentrates in such areas as conservation, classification, and seriation, all of which allows him to take into account and coordinate more than one aspect of reality at a time, which in turn fosters more adaptive knowledge of the physical world. Feffer accentuates the fact that an analogous decentering process occurs in the social realm, bringing with it enhanced interpersonal knowledge that is more adaptive than preceding cognitive limitations allowed. He developed a projective technique which is by now well known as the Role-Taking Test (RTT). It is a method applied to Schneiderman's Make a Picture Story. The latter consists of a series of domestic and community scenes accompanied by a set of cardboard human figures. The subject is required to place three figures in three different scenes and then make up a story for each arrangement. He is further expected to retell the basic story in each instance by shifting from the various perspectives of each of the characters in the stories. The test involves an attempt at ascertaining the extent to which a subject will decenter from the content of his own initial perspective as reflected in the basic story he had made up and from the immediate perceptual stimuli of the scene. The assignment becomes increasingly more complex as the subject shifts from perspective to perspective, for he must simultaneously maintain the continuity of the theme while at the same time embracing the limitation imposed by each new decentration or refocusing. Successfully accomplished, this results in balanced decentering.

In a series of papers, Feffer and his collaborators[8] applied the RTT to explore several hypotheses. In the 1959 paper he concludes that the RTT is a valid means for evaluating level of cognitive maturity, having found an association between a formal analysis of role-taking ability and an independent measure of cognitive development derived from the Rorschach Composite Index. The essence of the latter pertains to the subject's cognitive ability at differentiation and integration in organizing perceptual stimuli. In the 1960 paper, Feffer shifts from having used an adult population to utilizing children of various ages. Further, he compared their RTT scores to independent scores on exclusively Piagetian tasks such as conservation. In so doing he is dealing with the unitary construct of decentration as it cuts across both personal and impersonal realms. Feffer again concludes that the decentering concept as revealed in the RTT may validly serve as a criterion for inferring cognitive maturity. He bases this on the findings that there was a positive association between decentration in the RTT and the various Piagetian tasks utilized. Also, both role-taking and decentration were positively associated with advances in age. In general, as children grow older, their role-taking capacities increase, with especially marked advances noted between eight to nine years and ten to eleven.

It is in the 1966 paper that Feffer begins to direct his research toward demonstrating that a high level of perspective taking, facilitated by decentration, has significant implications for social adaptiveness, a belief he intimated in his early work. Prominent in the present discussion is the manner in which single centrations produce distortions, as opposed to balanced decentrations, which correct for distortions.

A balanced decentration is one in which two or more perspectives are taken into account simultaneously, allowing the individual to modify his intended behavior in relation to how he anticipates the other would react to it were it to be carried out. This notion strikes a chord of recognition resonating from the work of Mead, with which Feffer was certainly familiar.

For Feffer, optimal social interaction between two people proceeds when both are utilizing simultaneous decentering. Subjects who shift perspectives in the RTT but do not maintain continuity and consistency among the characters are said to be engaging in sequential decentering. Those who go from character to character in the story, alternating perspectives, while maintaining continuity and consistency, are engaged in simultaneous decentering.

Feffer paired thirty-six subjects into eighteen dyads, each matched for role-taking capacity as measured by the RTT. The subjects were undergraduate college students enrolled in a psychology course. A separate measure pertaining to the effectiveness of social interaction characterizing each dyad was then made. The task involved the indirect communication of a key word from one member of the dyad to the other by use of one-word association clues. The partner receiving the message was permitted to respond aloud by guessing at the one word which he thought was the correct response.

Feffer stresses that optimal effectiveness involves social cooperation as each participant attempts to anticipate the other and dovetails his responses to meet the requirements of the activity. Each takes into account several perspectives simultaneously. For example, the receiver must alter his future responses in relation to both his own former responses and the clues that have been offered to him already. The donor, of course, must consider his knowledge of the correct word, past responses from the receiver, and thoughts of how the receiver might respond to the next association clue. This in turn might alter what word he will select to convey.

Results of the research indicated that the dyads rated with higher RTT scores completed the password task with fewer clues and in less time than was required by those with lower RTT scores. The importance of this increases when compared to a variation of the task which eliminated the variable of social interaction, so that reciprocal adjustments as described above could not occur. In this variation there did not appear any significant correlation between RTT scores and successful completion of the task.

In the 1970 paper, Feffer presents a summary statement of the developmental stages in role-taking which his research uncovered. He states the following:

> Essentially three main patterns of response have emerged from the analysis of such role-taking productions. The first, typically evidenced at about six years of age, is characterized by uncorrected decentering, that is, by obvious discontinuity between all versions of the story. . . . A second pattern becomes predominant between seven and eight years of age and is characterized by a limited, fluctuating form of coordination between perspectives. Although each of the perspectives may be relatively consistent with the initial story, they are sequentially focused on with respect to one another. . . . The third pattern, which only becomes clearly evident at about nine years of age is characterized by a synthesis of the different perspectives and hence is considered as showing the simultaneous coordination indicative of the cognitive operation.[9]

An example of the first pattern would be an instance in which the child originally tells a story that has the father eagerly prepared to give his wife a birthday gift. Then, when specifically shifting from the general story to the perspective of the father, he is described as preoccupied with what will be served for dinner. In the second pattern, there may be a consistent shift from a father who is suggesting that the family go out for a walk to the son who excitedly inquires where they will go. The third pattern is relatively complex, entailing a dual shifting between internal and external orientations. A teacher may be described as feeling bad because he had to flunk a student, but he observes that the student did deserve it. Alternately, assuming the student's perspective, the student is described as feeling guilty because he did not do his assignments properly, but understanding that the teacher did what he had to do. There is a fine coordination of multiple perspectives in his final version of role-taking achievement.

Feffer's contribution is a substantial one and it is apparent that those who are highest in the type of perspective taking reflected in the RTT would be most likely to have the potential for resolving conflicts of competing claims amongst individuals in a just manner.

## FLAVELL'S INSTRUMENTAL MODEL OF PERSPECTIVISM

In a major work on the subject, John Flavell et al. provide an especially explicit definition of role-taking, as follows:

> The basic and essential ingredient of any sort of skill sequence in this area appears to be that process in which the individual somehow cognizes . . . certain attributes of another individual. The attributes in question are primarily of the type that could be described as inferential rather than directly perceptible, for example, the other's needs, his intentions, his opinions and beliefs, and his emotional, perceptual or intellectual capacities and limitations.[10]

Flavell did not set out to uncover causal antecedents, believing that, given the state of the field, this should be a task for future research. He sought, instead, to provide a developmental-descriptive account of perspectivism, which would observe the ontogenetic qualitative changes which occur as the child moves through the early and middle years, as well as adolescence.

Flavell conceives of role-taking activity as serving the function of promoting understanding of the other as an end in itself or of fostering communication and persuasion. It could be utilized on behalf of either cooperative or competitive behaviors. Since he emphasizes an instrumental function, he has carried his analysis a step beyond what is ordinarily encountered in the literature, to include the subskills employed in attaining the end goal of role-taking.

The model that Flavell generated from his studies contains the following components: existence, need, prediction, maintenance, and application.

By *existence*, he means to signify the subjects' fundamental recognition that one's own thoughts, feelings, and perceptions may not be the same as those another person experiences. It extends to an awareness that the knowledge two or more people may have of an identical object could differ with respect to thoughts, feelings, and perceptions, depending upon their perspective. Acquiring this level of knowing represents the basic shift from egocentric to nonegocentric. It does not include, however, the requisite skills to make the correct inferences about taking other people's perspective, which successful role-taking demands.

The *need* component highlights the fact that one may have the knowledge that other people's perspective could differ from his own, without having the awareness that a particular situation may call for invoking the role-taking capabilities at his command. An awareness of this need in appropriate situations facilitates calling into play the relevant skills.

*Prediction* is the exercise of the actual role-taking skills necessary to making accurate inferences about another's role attributes. The exact nature of these skills is not well understood. What has been firmly established, however, is that there are definite differences of a qualitative nature characterizing these skills accompanying age progression. Flavell has emphasized that there is a strong tendency for one's own point of view to preempt consciousness, even if correct inferences are made about another's role attributes.

Therefore, this tendency must be countered so that inferential knowledge about another may be retained sufficiently to accomplish the role-taking goal in any given situation. This is precisely what Flavell intends to highlight by including *maintenance* as an element of the model.

Assuming that one has successfully undergone the preceding aspects of role-taking activity, he must still possess a capacity for knowing how to apply his inferred and stably held knowledge to achieving the situational goal. For example, a subject may call forth the first four elements of the model in a communication task, but fail in the area of *application* because he lacks the skill required in the specific situation to verbally construct the exact message necessary for success at the task. Skills involved in the field of application will also develop qualitatively with age.

A point that Flavell seeks to accent is that a subject who fails in a role-taking task may be deficient in any one of the identified elements of the model. The researcher should, therefore, not simply make the globular assessment that the subject lacks role-taking capability, but should carry out an analysis to discover where in the total process, suggested by the model, the subject is lacking. Familiarity with Flavell's conceptualization of the full range of role-taking activities guided toward the instrumental achievement of specified goals should protect one against naive and overly simplistic views on perspectivism.

Once having formulated his model from the research conducted by him and his collaborators, Flavell then reflexively utilizes it to comment on their findings. The preschool child seems to lack a solid concept imparting knowledge of the existence of alternate perspectives held by others. Upon entering school, a knowledge of perspectivism seems evident among most children, but it is not as yet well developed. The neophyte in school does possess some abilities contingent upon the aspects of need, prediction, maintenance, and application, but these are minimal and tenuous at this early stage.

It is during middle childhood and adolescence that the most extensive and deepest changes are observed in role-taking, as well as in communication skills. The existence component is on firm ground by this time and the changes appear mostly in the subsequent categories.

The 1968 work of Flavell et al. has been broadly described and the major theoretical model derived from it presented. It is a rich treasure of meticulously detailed research which bears reading by the motivated scholar. The remaining material on Flavell in the present discussion will cite one study from his book because of its intrinsic value per se and also because of its comparative relevance to an earlier procedure instituted by Feffer, which has been examined. Following this, a later research project will be introduced to highlight its contribution to the gains made in adolescent role-taking ability.

One incisive method utilized in the study of role-taking was to present a series of seven cards, each depicting a scene, in a predetermined sequence to the subject. The ordered sequence clearly manifests a particular story line, which the child is asked by an experimenter to state. Then three of the cards are removed and those remaining clearly reflect a quite different story. A second experimenter enters the room and it becomes the task of the child to anticipate the story that this experimenter, never having seen all seven cards together, will tell on the basis of the four remaining cards. Unlike Feffer's Role-Taking Test the materials are not ambiguous and, hence, do not require a projective response. Of course, the possibility of projecting onto a situation always exists, no matter how well defined a situation may be. The point is that the structure of this task does not by its nature call forth a projective response, as in the case of the RTT. There is no way that the second experimenter, who has seen only the four cards, could logically know about the story contained in the seven cards, within the limits of the experiment. The responses of the subjects were divided into four categories. Basically, however, these could be dichotomized into subjects who persisted in providing a story founded upon their original perspective from the seven cards, which they ascribed to the second experimenter, and subjects who recognized that this experimenter, of necessity, had a different perspective based on the four cards and which could not logically coincide with the child's original perspective. The population studied consisted of 160 students, in eight groups of 20 each. The groups represented grades two through eight, plus grade eleven. There occurred a significant age trend in which more children increasingly acquired the ability to exclude the story version represented in their initial observation and to take the role of the second experimenter, hence correctly predicting that he would tell the story reflected in the four cards before him. The most significant quantitative shift among those acquiring this capability took place between the ages of eight and nine.

A conceptual analysis is revealing, for in the second part of the experiment both the child and the second experimenter are facing the four cards only. What prevents the child from immediately identifying the experimenter's perspective, since at the moment it appears to be his own as well? Flavell advances the notion that there is a force or pressure exerted upon the child who does not shift perspectives in this context to interpret his original story as an absolute rather than relative reality. His thinking lacks flexibility as his conception of the story line is irreversibly fused to the initial version of the seven cards and he cannot decentrate from that. The persistence of the former story now imposing itself upon the present situation is akin to intellectual realism, in which psychic properties are absolutized and externalized. In effect, Flavell is saying that the general limitations of preoperational thought constrict the child's role-taking ability and preclude the capacity to shift perspectives. Briefly, role-taking ability is integrally related to overall cognitive functioning and development.

Miller, Kessel, and Flavell, in "Thinking About Thinking," have conducted a study on social cognitive development which is particu-

larly instructive regarding the significant advances brought with age
through adolescence. The major theoretical observation made here is
that representational acts can be recursive, based on a nesting hierarchy of structures. This is in contrast to motor and perceptual acts.
For example, a person may observe another person who is looking at
him, but he cannot proceed to observe the undergirding perceptual
action which is part of that other person who is looking at him. In
contrast, on a plane of mental representation, there may exist a recursive structuring such as, "I think that you think that we think
that they think . . ." Conceivably this could go on indefinitely. Now,
it is essential to understand that the foregoing does not signify mere
mental gymnastics. Rather, it seems to be the case that attainment of
recursive thinking of this sort is found only among adolescents and
adults, carrying with it profound implications for role-taking competence and action strategies based upon it.

The study by Miller et al. did, in fact, demonstrate that recursive
thought develops in an invariant sequence. The subjects utilized in
their study were seventy two in number, ranging from grades one
through six. There were four basic steps in development observed
and even the youngest children in the study seemed to grasp the
first. The four invariant steps were referred to as contiguous, action,
one-loop recursion, and two-loop recursion. The procedure was to
show the subjects drawings designed to reflect various states from
among the four possibilities, thereby permitting those subjects who
could conceive of them to identify them from the test material stimuli.

The contiguous category simply depicts one person thinking about
another.

The action category involves one person thinking about another
person, who is carrying out a social interaction such as talking. This
is structurally more complex as one person is conceived as carrying
out an action within an action. That is, the thinker is said to be thinking about someone who is in turn carrying out the action of talking to
someone. One aspect is nested hierarchically within the other.

In the third category, one-loop recursion, the scenes depict a nesting of thinking itself. That is, person A is thinking about person B in
the act of thinking about person C. This constitutes a mental act of
thinking about thinking. In this case one person may be the object of

two others who are said to be thinking about him. The third person is embedded in the thought processes of the second and the first, whereas the second and the third persons are embedded in the thought process of the first. Hence, a teacher may be thinking about a student who is thinking about his mother. In this illustration the mother is embedded in the thought process of both the student and the teacher in a nesting hierarchy. Similarly, the mother and the student are embedded in the thought process of the teacher. Miller et al. suggest that this capacity for one-loop recursive activity may be distinctly facilitated by the development of the Piagetian grouping 1, which is the composition of classes. This category of one-loop recursive skill does emerge in middle childhood and a conceptual analysis seems to reveal a structural similarity to classification competence.

The final category in this developmental sequence of social cognition, a two-loop recursion, takes us one step further. Here we have a situation in which, for example, the teacher is thinking that the student is thinking of his mother thinking of his father. In brief, there occurs thinking about thinking about thinking. Miller et al. point out that while this is structurally more complex than the developments of previous stages, its occurrence in everyday life is likely to be found much less frequently. As the fourth category is the last of an invariant sequence and the oldest children in the study were approximately twelve years old, it is probable that it owes its presence to the emergence of formal operations.

In closing, Miller et al. relate their work specifically to role-taking as follows:

> It is not surprising to find that the understanding of recursive thought is not nearly complete by the sixth grade. This finding is roughly in accord with a previous study of role-taking activity . . . in which game strategies requiring complex inferences about recursive interpersonal thought did not become common until adolescence. Understanding that thinking possesses a recursive, "wheel-within-wheels" property may well be a prerequisite for these complex role-taking-type inferences found in adolescence.[11]

Miller et al. in the above statement are referring to complex guessing games that have been utilized in the research on role-taking which involve invoking anticipatory strategies (i.e., I am anticipating, that he is anticipating, that I am anticipating that . . . ) leading to the modification of one's behavior as it would otherwise have occurred. The relation of this current research to Mead's early theory of symbolic interaction is unmistakable.

## SELMAN'S SOCIAL PERSPECTIVISM AND MORAL DEVELOPMENT

The extensive contribution of Robert L. Selman to the field of social perspectivism is creative and powerful. He has drawn freely from Baldwin, Mead, Piaget, Feffer and Flavell. Of greatest relevance is the intrinsic connection between his work and that of Kohlberg's theory of sociomoral knowledge. Selman, like Kohlberg, built his work upon the Piagetian structural-developmental foundation. Therefore, it will not be surprising to learn that Selman conceives of role-taking as developing through an increasingly more complex hierarchy of invariant stages involving a process through which each succeeding stage becomes more adequate and inclusive as it represents a reorganization of concepts from the preceding stage. The underlying structural development of social perspective taking, which constitutes the central motif to Selman's work, has been pursued in two distinct but related directions. It has been applied to the domains of moral reasoning[12] and interpersonal concepts.[13] Selman's view is that perspective taking is more fundamental than either of those two areas and exists as a necessary but not sufficient condition in relation to them. Because of its more immediate relevance to the subject of this dissertation, emphasis will be given to Selman's theoretical position and empirical findings regarding the nature of perspective taking and its correspondence with stages of moral reasoning.

Crucial to appreciating Selman's and Kohlberg's work is grasping the phenomenological aspect inherent in both positions. Whether it is social or moral reasoning that is the focus of attention, the essential point in relation to any particular child is how he views the world in these two domains. It is only by eliciting from the child, or even the adult, his specific conceptions and underlying reasons for holding them, that light will be cast upon the manner in which he organizes and comprehends his sociomoral matrix.

Selman is clear in his contention that role-taking is not a single skill which one either does or does not possess. The adoption of such a static conception by some researchers may account for the discrepant reports in the literature regarding the age at which it appears. By assuming the view that perspective taking is a process of progressive structural development, the important question becomes what form it takes at different levels. Although it may be true that the presence of a primitive role-taking sensitivity may be observed as early as age two or three, as maintained by some, there is no way that this can be held to even remotely approximate the qualitative level of perspective taking found in adolescence. Further, the view that perspectivism is characterized by qualitative changes runs counter to conceiving of it as a quantitative phenomenon based on additive pieces of social information. The critical function involved in the process is the promotion of comprehending the relations that obtain between one's own perspective and those of others. Of special interest at each level of development is how the child differentiates between his own and other's perspectives, as well as the manner in which these are coordinated by him. Also of concern is knowing how any given level signifies an advance in differentiation and coordination over the previous level and how it remains limited compared to the structural organization that may succeed it. Acquiring this dual perspective of past and future will deepen understanding of the present level.

A brief description of the levels through which perspective taking evolves is in order. They make this appearance in an invariant sequence as follows:

*Level 0:* Egocentric social perspective taking (ages 3–6). An ability to recognize simple affect in others is manifest. Nevertheless, a child during this period confuses his own subjectivity with others'. He is likely to believe that when in the same situation another person will feel as he does. Hence, there is no differentiation between his own perspective and that of other people.

*Level 1:* Subjective social perspective taking (ages 6–8). At this time there is an awareness of the distinct subjectivity of each person's own viewpoint. The child recognizes that even when in the same situation as another person, the other may construe it differently than he does. He recognizes further that access to varying information will result in different subjective interpretations. However, he cannot simultaneously entertain both his own and another person's viewpoint. He also lacks the ability to see himself from the perspective of another person.

*Level 2:* Self-reflective perspective taking (ages 8–10). There now develops a reciprocal understanding that just as the child himself can view the other as a subject, it is also true that the other can view the child as a subject. This awareness that the other can view him as a subject will influence his actions toward the other. The child can also now view himself through the perspective of another. The advance encompassed at this level is limited by the fact that the reflections involved take place sequentially and, therefore, the child is still locked into a dyadic situation.

*Level 3:* Third-person perspective taking (ages 10–12). There occurs a mutuality of role-taking. The child becomes aware that each person in a dyadic situation has the capability of a simultaneous knowledge of his own and the other's subjectivity. He can transcend the immediate dyadic situation to adopt an abstract third-person perspective which permits observation of his own interaction with the other and their mutual subjectivity.

*Level 4:* Qualitative systems level of perspective taking (ages 12–15). The young person by now has generated a *generalized other* perspective which he knows he shares with others. It is a perspective that others in the community may also hold regardless of their social position. It is comprised of an integration of communally shared values, attitudes, and beliefs. There is now an idea of a social system perspective which goes beyond the abstract third-person perspective of level 3 that observes only a specific dyadic interaction. Social conceptions now include knowledge that relationships can exist at varying levels such as in a state of being lovers, best friends, friends, or simply acquaintances.

*Level 5:* Symbolic interaction perspective taking (ages 15+). The relativity of socially rooted perspectives is discerned. A perspective which goes beyond the confines of any given society in which one happens to find himself can be adopted.

Selman rejects the notion that moral judgment is merely a special case of these perspective taking levels applied to the moral realm. Although the former is necessary to moral reasoning, the latter calls into play components that are distinctive to it. A recent report by Selman, "The Relation of Social Perspective-Taking," attempts to offer longitudinally based data to support the fundamental hypothesis that perspectivism is a necessary but not sufficient condition for moral development. The report is based upon a massive collection and analysis of material from longitudinal interviews with ten of the original subjects in the Kohlberg study. The subjects were ten years old when the study by Kohlberg began and Selman utilized the same material that was accumulated by Kohlberg over the years as the young people continued in the study. Material from five interviews with each of the ten subjects was examined and scored for perspective taking level. There were a total of forty-seven interviews (three had been missed) spanning five different ages that the subjects passed through during the course of the study. A significant age progression was documented in regard to levels of perspective taking. For example, only 10 percent of the children at age ten demonstrated level 3 as their predominant level of perspective taking. By age thirteen, this figure had risen to 70 percent. At age nineteen one subject remained at level 3, while the remaining subjects had all passed beyond it. At age twenty-two all subjects had gone beyond the third level. Furthermore, the data confirmed the invariant hypothesis. There was not a single instance in which a subject went from being scored at one level to a lower level after the passage of time. The direction of change evidenced was invariably from a lower level to a higher level and there were no signs of any subject having skipped over a level. Finally, each of the forty-seven interviews was analyzed and scored from the standpoint of correspondence between perspective level and moral stage. There was not a single case in which moral stage was higher than perspective level. In 54 percent ($N = 25$) of the cases a parallel correspondence between stages in the two areas was noted. The perspective taking level was found to be one higher than stage of moral reasoning in 46 percent ($N = 22$) of the cases. If there were not a necessary but not sufficient relation obtaining, then one would expect to find at least some instances in which moral stage would be more advanced than perspective taking.

Selman, citing the work of Byrne, "Role-Taking in Adolescence," in the same report presents an additional study testing once again the necessary but not sufficient condition hypothesis. This cross-sectional study utilized a population of fifty-six males evenly divided among ages ten, thirteen, sixteen, and adulthood. Unlike the previous study, Byrne employed two independent sources of measurement, whereas Selman had derived his scores from the same data base. Special means were devised by Byrne to test perspective taking with a view toward assessing the levels specific to adolescence and beyond. Moral stages, as in Selman's study, were defined in terms of Kohlberg's theory. Results,[14] once correlations were tabulated, revealed that twenty-four cases were parallel in development, in twenty-five cases perspective taking was one level higher than moral stage and in five cases it was two higher. In one case moral stage appeared to be one stage higher than perspective taking. The last statement would seem to be a logical impossibility if the theory is correct. However, in the light of Selman's evidence and the balance of Byrne's own findings, the greater likelihood is that it signifies an error in measurement.

Attempting to formulate a position statement in the relation between the dimensions under consideration, Selman suggests, "The structural core of the moral stages refers to the way in which the subject orients to the conflicting claims of all participants in the moral dilemma. The form by which one considers the claims of oneself and others presupposes the prior form of understanding the relationship of the prespectives of oneself and other." Hence, perspective taking is always necessary but never sufficient for parallel moral reasoning.

## CONCLUDING REMARKS

The twin concepts of egocentrism and role-taking, because of the prominent contribution they make to an understanding of moral development, have been examined at length. Some of Kohlberg's own comments on the nature and origins of role-taking have been introduced and the early relevant work of Baldwin, Mead, and Piaget has been presented. The contemporary work of Feffer, Flavell, and Selman has been formulated, with a special emphasis upon Selman's social perspective taking levels and their relationship to moral stages.

Although everything that has been covered in this chapter may be subsumed under the broad category of social cognition, that field is too extensive to have justifiably included here all that goes under that classification. There do exist, however, two recent comprehensive and excellent literature reviews on social cognition, Shantz's "Development of Social Cognition," and Chandler's "Social Cognition." Finally, Kurdek has made an exhaustive review of the literature which specifically covers the relationship between perspective taking and moral development. He has emerged from his search with a modest but forward-looking thrust, as he states:

There are enough conceptual and methodological problems in the existing body of literature . . . to conclude that the relationship between perspective taking and moral development has not been adequately assessed. The venture of searching for the cognitive components of various facets of children's moral development . . . remains defensible and perspective taking ability is the front-running candidate for the position.[15]

# Chapter Four

# The Stage Theory of
# Moral Development

Lawrence Kohlberg (1927–    ) is the leading contemporary figure in the field of sociocognitive moral development. His work represents a profound extension and refinement of Piaget's early book on moral judgment. Research currently being conducted in the field is largely a derivative of his complex system. Literally scores of articles critical of his work have appeared in the literature and this phenomenon in itself is suggestive of the monumental impact of his work. Kohlberg has not been insensitive to criticisim and it is known that he has been engaged in an ongoing process of revising his methods and formulations when encountering valid critical commentary or new findings that demand reconciliation with a prior position.

The first portion of this chapter will be organized around a general characterization of Kohlberg's moral psychology and philosophy. It will be followed by an in-depth examination of the six stages of moral development based upon his major longitudinal study and confirmed by cross-cultural research. In the following chapter the discussion will be carried forth by focusing upon several major questions which inevitably arise in the context of Kohlberg's work. Serious criticism will be reserved for a separate chapter following the exposition of this material.

To avoid misunderstanding, it is essential from the outset to be clear on what is implied by Kohlberg's use of the term "moral stage." It does not refer simply to an application of cognitive reasoning to the moral realm. Moral reasoning involves structural development which is specific to its own domain even though, as we shall see in the next chapter, cognitive operations constitute a necessary, but not sufficient condition for moral development. Further, a moral stage does not automatically signify anything about behavior. The relationship between stage and action is a separate issue and it, too, will be explored subsequently. The stage concept is utilized by Kohlberg to denote a moral judgment. It is prescriptive or normative in that it deals with what a subject thinks is right and, therefore, concerns what *ought* to be. Stages are derived by posing anecdotal conflict situations to subjects and asking them *not* how *they* would behave in that situation, but about the behavior of the characters in the situation. Conceptions pertaining to rights and duties, implying *values* in these areas, are then elicited. The dilemmas presented to the subjects are designed to place obedience to authority and law in opposition to individual rights and human welfare. Once a subject has made a moral judgment, the underlying reasoning that brought it forth is explored in the interview. It is not the content of the judgment that determines what stage a subject is at, but the form of covert moral reasoning that had led him to the position he adopted. It is theoretically possible for each of six subjects to make the same overt judgment about a moral dilemma while at the same time each being at a different stage from the others. Similarly two different subjects may make opposing moral judgments and yet be at the same stage. This is because a structural analysis of the underlying reasoning is the stage determinant and not the content of the judgment. An elaboration of the actual stages, appearing later in this chapter, will clarify this essential point further.

In a very significant way, Kohlberg's stage theory bears a greater resemblance to Piaget's cognitive stage theory than it does to the moral theory of Piaget. Kohlberg's stages are held to be universal and to follow an invariant sequence of development in all cultures. Each subsequent stage represents a reorganization and synthesis of the elements in the preceding stage and is generative of a qualitatively different mode of structural moral reasoning. Piaget did not make the claim that the stages in his moral theory meet formal stage criteria, whereas he has decisively made that claim for the development of logical operations. In passing through Kohlberg's stages, one person may move through them more slowly than another, but it would not be predicted that anyone could move through them by reversing the order of any of the stages nor could any of the stages be skipped.⟧ Also, a person would not be expected to regress to a previous stage. Passage through all six stages is not likely, however, and in the United States among urban middle-class people the dominant mode of moral reasoning is at stage 4. Stating that a person is at a particular stage indicates that approximately half or more of his moral reasoning is grounded in the defining nature of that stage. It also implies that the balance of his moral conceptions is likely to be divided between one stage higher and one stage lower. Therefore, it should be obvious that a person will not always exercise moral reasoning at his basic stage and certainly not the highest stage at which he is capable of reasoning.

Kohlberg rejects the notion that moral judgment is founded upon an internalization by the growing child of cultural rules inculcated through verbal transmission, the administration of punishment, or identification with a model. The cultural moral relativism implied in internalization theories runs counter to his quite fundamental assertion that stage development is universal. The content of a particular culture will, of course, become grist for the structural mill, but will not alter essentially the development of modes of moral reasoning. ⟦The cultural environment will have a significant impact upon the rate of development as a function of the role-taking opportunities it provides, but this will have no effect on the universality and invariance of the sequence.⟧ Cross-cultural research supporting Kohlberg's position has been conducted in Canada, Turkey, India, Martinique, Taiwan, Mexico, and Israel. Studies have been made with both middle-class and lower-class groups, as well as with children from preliterate and semiliterate cultures. Kohlberg has also found that neither a particular religious faith nor atheism will have a bearing upon the invariant sequence. This has been investigated not only with Catholics, Protestants, and Jews, but with Buddhists and Moslems as well.

There are two central concepts which function throughout the developing process and which warrant citation prior to progressing to an exploration of the actual stages. One is the concept of equilibration which Kohlberg has borrowed from Piaget and which has been discussed in chapter 1. It is the dynamic mechanism utilized to explain stage transitions and will recur with still further elaboration in later portions of this book. The other is the concept of differentiation and integration, which has been adopted from the organismic theory of Werner, stated in his *Comparative Psychology of Mental Development*. It posits that in the earliest phase of development there exists a globular and undifferentiated state which in time becomes differentiated, with the elements forming a hierarchic integration. The common biological example often cited is the one cell dividing into many cells which begin to interrelate functionally, while going on to organize into hierarchical structures. An example from cognitive development, which also has a biological foundation, is the development of classification. Early classification schemes are globular and undifferentiated. All furry animals may be classified by the very young child as "doggie." The perception of furry animals is globular and undifferentiated. In time differentiation occurs and the child has classification structures to distinguish among dogs, cows, foxes and other animals. These are organized into a hierarchy under the generic class of animals. In fact, the taxonomy of primates, including humans, which anthropologists have devised constitutes an extraordinarily complex hierarchy of finely differentiated elements. It is also the case in moral judgment that each stage represents greater differentiation and integration than the previous stage. The value of life, for example, is not differentiated from material wealth at stage 1. The differentiation occurs by stage 2, at which time there is a lack of differentiation between personal desire and the value of life, which does not become differentiated until stage 3. The process continues throughout development. Not only is property differentiated from life in value terms, but a later development is the differentiation between human life and animal life. Implicit in the value differentiations is a hierarchy, with human life valued over animal life and animal life valued over property.

## THE MORAL DEVELOPMENTAL SEQUENCES

Kohlberg commenced a longitudinal study on moral development with his doctoral dissertation, "The Development of Modes of Moral Thinking." The dissertation was completed in 1958; the study is still in progress. The results were first reported in the literature in 1963 with "The Development of Children's Orientation." The monumental scope of this study imparts a degree of credence that is simply unattainable in nonlongitudinal studies. I will first present a characterization of Kohlberg's comments on the original work and then proceed to discuss the stages in order of their ontogenetic appearance. In discussing the stages, however, the material brought to bear will not be confined to Kohlberg's earliest statements, but will range across the years that have followed as well.

The population of the study originally resided in the suburbs of Chicago. There were seventy-two boys divided into three age groups: ten, thirteen, and sixteen years. In each group one-half was from the upper middle class and the other half from working to lower middle class. Each age group had comparable IQs. Ten moral dilemmas were discussed on a hypothetical plane with each subject during a two-hour tape-recorded clinical interview. The idea for conducting the research, it is acknowledged, was derived from Piaget's fifth book, *The Moral Judgment of the Child.* It was the task, in each dilemma, to resolve the inherent conflict. The choice was always between an act that would comply with sociolegal rules or an act that would violate the rules but serve human needs or the welfare of others, which would be neglected by obedience. Analyzing the content of the responses, i.e., the choice of which act should be carried out, proved unfruitful. The analysis of the underlying reason for the choice is what turned out to be revealing.

Analysis of the raw data from the interviews produced a pattern of six stages of moral development, reflected in thirty general aspects of morality inherent in the verbal responses of the subjects. Together these led to the construction of a typology with 180 cells (i.e., 30 x 6). The aspects included such categories as punishment, rights, and motivation. Each aspect could be considered from the standpoint of which stage it corresponded to. For example, in assessing a statement that had a motivational aspect, if the motivation for a particular choice of action pivoted around the theme of "disapproval by others," then it would be scored in a specific column for motivation in the cell reserved for stage 3, because that stage is defined by its emphasis upon good relations and approval. If the motivational aspect had been "punishment by another," then it would have been entered in the cell reserved for stage 1, which is defined by its emphasis upon physical consequences and avoiding punishment. All of the moral ideas conveyed during the interview were thus analyzed according to aspect and stage. It was then possible to ascertain what percentage of all statements by each subject was at a certain stage. Although dealing with thirty aspects, a rather heterogeneous array, there was an impressive degree of stage consistency, which Kohlberg has viewed as a strong supporting argument for his position that moral stage theory constitutes structured wholes and not isolated skills. The typology provided a profile on each boy and the computation of percentages yielded information on which stage of moral development he was at. The original results indicated that stages 1 and 2 decline with age, whereas there occurs an increase in the appearance of stages 3 and 4 until thirteen years. Stages 4 and 5 increase until age sixteen. Kohlberg was to discover later that moral development continues for considerably longer than he originally concluded. His instructors in this vital lesson were to be these same boys as they grew older, many of them going to college and subsequently graduating. (In this longitudinal study, N=53.)

Kohlberg believed that he had found a basis in his data for dividing the six stages into three natural levels, each one comprised of two stages. Hence, level 1 was comprised of stages 1 and 2, level 2 of stages 3 and 4, and level 3 of stages 5 and 6. There appeared to be a higher correlation between the two stages grouped within any one level than between any stage within one level and a stage in another level. The three levels and six stages will be presented, following this summary statement by Kohlberg from his first published work.

> From the internalization view of the moralization process, these age changes in modes of moral thought would be interpreted as successive acquisitions or internalizations of cultural moral concepts. Our six types of thought would represent six patterns of verbal morality in the adult culture which are successively absorbed as the child grows more verbally sophisticated.
>
> In contrast, we have advocated the developmental interpretation that these types of thought represent structures emerging from the interaction of the child with his social environment, rather than directly reflecting external structures given by the child's culture. . . . While these successive bases of a moral order do spring from the child's awareness of the external world, they also represent active processes of organizing or ordering his world.[1]

It is clear that Kohlberg embraces an active organism model, which holds that the growing person constructs and reconstructs his own moral knowledge out of exchanges with social beings in the environment.⟩

## THREE LEVELS OF MORAL DEVELOPMENT

In "Moral Stages and Moralization," a recent overview and update of his own work, Kohlberg has presented the three levels in relation to social perspectives, which I believe is in itself a commentary on the significance he accords the latter. However, he distinguishes what he refers to as a sociomoral perspective from the role-taking stages of Selman, believing it is a broader concept underlying both role-taking and moral judgment.

The preconventional level (stages 1 and 2) is one at which the individual does not yet understand society's rules and expectations. In relation to the self they remain external. He neither comprehends the grounds for their being nor does he have any sense of having participated in designing them. His is a concrete individual perspective. Paramount in his considerations are his own personal interests and sometimes those of isolated individuals other than himself. Responsiveness to rules at this level is based upon anticipated physical or hedonistic consequences of his behavior. There is a deference to the superior power of authorities. Children under nine years have rarely gone beyond this level and some adolescents may still be found to be at level 1. Kohlberg points out that it is also a prevalent level among adolescents and adults who have committed criminal offences.

The conventional level (stages 3 and 4) encompasses the majority of people, adolescents and adults, in all societies. People at this level advocate support of the law precisely because it is the law. Rules and expectations are identified with or internalized by the self. Hence, the rule of authority is no longer experienced as an external imposition and compliance has a more volitional character. This flows from a member-of-society perspective. The perspective no longer is a concrete individual one, but instead the individual's interests are secondary to the group's needs, welfare, and outlook. The individual at this level goes beyond mere compliance, seeking to actively maintain and justify the social order. A sense of loyalty is a strong feature at this level. The individual enjoys a sense of shared membership in the group.

The postconventional level (stages 5 and 6) is not arrived at before age twenty and even among an adult population relatively few people ever achieve it. The acceptance of society's rules is founded upon the individual's own capacity to construct and comprehend the general principles from which the rules derive. In time of conflict, convention is subordinated to principle. Kohlberg views this level as predicated upon a prior-to-society perspective. Paradoxically there is a return to an individual outlook rather than an unquestioning identification with the social group. However, it has a distinctively different quality from the individualism of the preconventional level. In Kohlberg's own words:

> The individual point of view taken at the postconventional level . . . can be universal; it is that of *any rational moral individual.* Aware of the member-of-society perspective, the postconventional person questions and redefines it in terms of an individual moral perspective, so that social obligations are defined in ways that can be justified to any moral individual. An individual's commitment to basic morality or moral principles is seen as preceding, or being necessary for, his taking society's perspective or accepting society's laws and values. Society's laws and values, in turn, should be ones which any reasonable person could commit himself to-whatever his place in society and whatever society he belongs to.[2]

Seen in light of the above it would be expected that there would be a greater consistency of moral choices among people at the postconventional level because of the rational universality underpinning them than among people at lower levels. This is what Kohlberg claims to happen and he refers to it as a "probabilistic tendency" for people at the higher stages of moral development to reach consensual agreement.

Kohlberg makes an important point in cautioning against identifying a person as being at the postconventional level solely because he may make a judgment based on individual conscience and what he insists is morally right in opposition to the established order. It is entirely possible that such a person may be identifying with the rules of a subgroup which he accepts with as little question as any other conventional-level person who, however, has identified with the wider social order. It is always the source and nature of one's moral reasoning that we must know to determine the structural level or stage.

It is perhaps useful to reflect upon the three levels from the stand-point of individuals' attitudes toward the law. Briefly, when the pre-conventional child advocates obedience to the law it is because harm may come to him if he doesn't obey it or good will come to him if he does obey it. When the conventional youngster supports the law it is because he perceives it as necessary to the preservation of good rela-tionships and social order. Lastly, when the postconventional adoles-cent or adult is found embracing the law it is because he believes it to be based upon principles which safeguard individual rights.

Within any given level, the second stage is found to be more highly organized and mature in relation to its general perspective than the stage first entered into when arriving at that level. In viewing the shifts from one level to another we see that the self of the preconven-tional individual decenters from his own personal interests as he moves onward to the conventional level. In turn, in order to ac-complish the passage from the conventional level to the postconven-tional level, the individual must decenter from the perspective of soci-ety. His widening perspective, as the self disengages from the environmental and cultural embeddedness, requires an increasing capacity for abstract thinking and provides greater adequacy of moral reasoning.

## SIX STAGES OF MORAL
## DEVELOPMENT

As the stages we are about to examine were based upon subjects' responses to stories containing moral conflicts it would be instructive at this point to cite the three illustrations that appear below.

*Story 1.* In Europe, a woman was near death from a kind of cancer. There was one drug that the doctors thought might save her. It was a form of radium that a druggist in the same town had recently discovered. The drug was expensive to make, but the druggist was charging ten times what the drug cost him to make. He paid $200 for the radium and charged $2,000 for a small dose of the drug. The sick woman's husband, Heinz, went to everyone he knew to bor-row the money, but he could only get together about $1,000 which is half of what it cost. He told the druggist that his wife was dying and asked him to sell it cheaper or let him pay later. But the druggist said, "No, I discovered the drug and I'm going to make money from it." So Heinz gets desperate and considers breaking into the man's store to steal the drug for his wife.

Story 2. Heinz did break into the store and got the drug. Watching from a distance was an off-duty police officer, Mr. Brown, who lived in the same town as Heinz and knew the situation Heinz was in. Mr. Brown ran over to try to stop Heinz, but Heinz was gone by the time Mr. Brown reached the store. Mr. Brown wonders whether he should look for Heinz and arrest him.

Story 3. Joe is a fourteen-year-old boy who wanted to go to camp very much. His father promised him he could go if he saved up the money himself. So Joe worked hard at his paper route and saved up the $40 it cost to go to camp and a little more besides. But just before camp was going to start, his father changed his mind. Some of his friends decided to go on a special fishing trip, and Joe's father was short of the money it would cost. So he told Joe to give him the money he had saved from the paper route. Joe didn't want to give up going to camp so he thinks of refusing to give his father the money.[3]

Once a story is presented to a subject, the investigator poses a series of pertinent questions about it and probes the respondent's answers. For example, in the first story, the subject is asked whether Heinz should steal the drug and the reasons behind the respondent's decision are then pursued. He is further asked whether Heinz's feelings toward his wife should influence his course of action and whether the prescribed action should be any different if the woman is a stranger to Heinz. Questions are posed regarding the law in the second situation and in general with a focus upon obedience. In the third story, the questions involve relationships, promises, and property rights. The subject's responses to stories of this type and their accompanying questions becomes the raw data from which an individual's stage of moral development is assessed.

## Stage 1: Heteronomous Morality

The defining feature of this stage is the individual's conception of right as being obedient to the power holders. Those in authority have a position enabling them to impose punishments upon those who disobey, hence obedience is subscribed to by stage 1 children because it will help to avoid punishment and other adverse consequences.

There is no vision of a moral order which must be maintained through punishment as necessary to accomplish that end. Hence, a notion of right is arrived at by anticipating the physical consequences of the act, irrespective of any other consideration. It is not the case that the child has no realization that there is a right and wrong at this embryonic stage, but that his notion of it pivots around the desire to avoid punishment. There is an old familiar phrase, "Might makes right," which carries something of the central meaning of this stage. The imprint of preoperational thought is upon this stage, as there is a distorting egocentrism in the child's centration upon only one aspect of the situation. The value of life during stage 1 is not differentiated from an individual's material possessions. Therefore, moral judgments regarding the value of any one person's life will be heavily influenced by his wealth.

There is obviously a sharp departure in Kohlberg's interpretation of this stage from that of Piaget's. Where Piaget emphasizes the child's emotional bond producing unilaterial respect toward the adult, Kohlberg does not. He suggests that in Piaget's view anticipated punishment is important because it signals to the child what the respected adult will or will not approve. Kohlberg found neither respect for adults nor an attitude of rules as sacred in children of this stage.

### Stage 2: Individualism and Instrumental Purpose and Exchange

In originally reporting his findings, Kohlberg observed that his stage 1 coincided with Piaget's stage of heteronomy and that stage 2 coincided with the autonomous stage in Piaget's work. However, it is frequently suggested that some elements of heteronomy as described by Piaget extend from stages 1 to 4 in Kohlberg's system, whereas elements of autonomy may be found ranging from stages 2 to 6.

The child's conception of right at stage 2 is essentially one of stark reciprocity. An exactly equal exchange of goods or favors seems to be the guiding light of this stage. Until recently the prevalent terminology for this stage was "instrumental hedonism." Doing something for another is right because he will repay you in some way now or later. Leaving someone alone is right, because then he will leave you alone. In a religious context, Kohlberg reports one child as saying a person should be good to God because then He will be good to the person. Reciprocity at this stage does not flow from a respect for the rights or

dignity of the other, but merely from a pragmatic expectation of receiving similar treatment. There appears a naive egalitarian outlook
with an accompanying dimunition of any sense that adults may be
morally superior.

A growing awareness of the relativism of each person's own needs
and perspective is now manifest. The hallmark of this stage is pursuing one's self interests and obtaining rewards, tempered only by a
pragmatic concept of fairness as equal exchange. Of paramount concern is having one's own needs fulfilled. The relativism of perspectives and reciprocity of this stage are the aspects that link it with
Piaget's autonomous stage. However, the full flowering of Kohlberg's
stages of development will take the growing person very far from this
as he constructs moral knowledge of a much higher order.

### Stage 3: Mutual Interpersonal Expectations, Relationships, and Interpersonal Conformity

The child now goes beyond strict equality to equity. Role-taking invokes taking into account the feelings and intentions of others. A
conception of right is geared to meeting the expectations of friends
and family. Loyalty and affiliation become of the utmost importance.
The Golden Rule is now exercised as the individual will place himself
in the other person's shoes to determine what is fair and desirable.
Kohlberg distinguishes this type of role-taking ability as imaginative
reciprocity in constrast to exchange reciprocity which is characteristic of stage 2. A concern for others is expressed. A desire to receive
praise and avoid blame will influence the judgment of what constitutes right and wrong action. Kohlberg refers to this sometimes as
the "Good-boy/Nice-girl" stage. One is motivated to observe rules in
order to maintain relationships. The individual's conception of right
at this stage is limited to people within his own circle and does not
extend to a broad societal level, encompassing both known and unknown members of the larger social group. It is at this stage, however, that the child is aware in interpersonal relationships that the
other will make a judgment about him based on his behavior. This
new role-taking ability will enable him to modify his intended behavior on the basis of how he anticipates the other might respond to it.
This capacity both allows the child to construct a new view of what
constitutes the right and at the same time helps him to fulfill what is
prescribed by it.

## Stage 4: Social System and Conscience

The scope of this stage encompasses the complete network of the entire society. There is a sense of obligation to obey laws and perform duties. Laws are construed as necessary to maintain society. The allegiance to following laws now springs from a conception of a moral order which goes beyond one's own circle of friends and relatives. The level of abstraction required at this stage is greater, for the notion of justice is based upon legislation issuing from government and is expected to apply to all people in the land without exception. To maintain the social order, conformity to the laws is demanded. This, of course, precludes deviation and diversity. The conservation of laws is emphasized and change is deemphasized.

Kohlberg provides an incisive comment on the main features of this stage:

> Stage 4 positive reciprocity is exchange of reward for effort or merit, not interpersonal exchange of goods or service. Negative reciprocity is even more clearly centered on the social system: vengeance is the right of society and is conceived not as vengeance but as "paying your debt to society." The equality element of justice appears primarily in terms of the uniform and regular administration of the law, and as equity in an order of merit. Social inequality is allowed where it is reciprocal to effort, moral conformity, and talent, but unequal favoring of the "idle" and "immoral," poor, students, etc., is strongly rejected.[4]

The majority of adults in most societies are at this stage. Kohlberg's description of it is not intended as a disparagement. He believes that it is a considerable advance over previous stages, that it is not merely an internalization of society's rules and taboos, and that in light of the relatively mature role-taking ability involved it is rooted cognitively in a fairly deep structure.

## Stage 5: Social Contract or Utility and Individual Rights

Discussion of this stage will open with a caveat. Although it is customary to present the traditional six stages without qualification, the fact is that since first identifying these stages, a considerable amount of attention has been devoted to the transition between stages 4 and 5. It is an especially critical juncture, since comparatively few people do progress to the postconventional level, and yet it is at this point that heteronomy is surpassed and genuinely principled moral reasoning emerges. To avoid muddying the waters, however, until familiarity with the basic stages has been acquired, I shall defer discussion of stage 4B.

It has been observed that the Piagetian moral characteristics of intentionality, reciprocity, and relativism appear in the developmental sequence prior to the postconventional level. Therefore, the defining features of principled thinking to be found in stages 5 and 6 must go beyond these characteristics, at least beyond them as they appear in conventional level forms.

Stage 4 moral reasoning concentrates on maintaining the status quo. Stage 5 is defined by a qualitatively different conception of justice attuned to the necessity of changing unjust laws. This moral vision is possible because of the prior-to-society perspective which the person at this stage is able to adopt. A perspective from this angle informs the mind that laws do not exist to be obeyed but to protect the rights of individuals and enhance the general welfare. A law that does not embody and assist in fulfilling a human right and which, in fact, runs counter to it must be changed. A democratic society is the natural outgrowth of stage 5 moral thinking. There exists in it a theoretically fair procedure for effecting change and it is recourse to this procedural mechanism which the stage 5 person will advocate when confronted with an unjust law. Hence, there is a legalistic orientation founded upon the social contract. It is not that there is any disrespect for law, but rather that the source of the respect is a knowledge of the purpose law is intended to fulfill. Therefore, when it fails to meet the standard set for it by the stage 5 person, then the grounds for changing it are clear and rational. Kohlberg formulates his view:

> There is clear awareness of the relativism of personal values and opinions and a corresponding emphasis upon procedural rules for reaching consensus. Aside from what is constitutionally and democratically agreed upon, the right is a matter of personal values and opinion. The result is an emphasis upon the legal point of view, but with an emphasis upon the possibility of changing law in terms of rational consideration of social utility. . . . Outside the legal realm, free agreement is the binding element of obligation.[5]

Kohlberg has pointed out the fact that not all moral conflicts are those between society's rules or interests and the egoistic impulses of the individual, which must be restrained. There may exist, and often does, conflict between two valid alternatives. Kohlberg's stories are designed to accentuate this type of dilemma and it is at stage 5 that the person becomes most accutely aware of this. Previously there is either an ignorance of the true nature of the conflict or an evasion of it. The stage 5 moral thinker recognizes it, faces it squarely, and attempts a genuinely rational resolution. The stage 4 thinker tends to view maintaining law and order as defending against the outsiders who do not comply or show proper respect for law. The stage 5 thinker in contrast is concerned with *just* procedural mechanisms that will extend across the range of all citizens to encompass suspected and even convicted criminals, whose rights must also be protected. There does not exist the same dichotomy between conforming insiders and nonconforming outsiders at stage 5 as there is at stage 4. The rights of any two citizens or of a single citizen and the general welfare may legitimately clash and the task is to seek a rational method for resolving the conflict which will be just. Kohlberg believes that a constitutional democracy provides the organization to achieve this. Implicit in the arrangement is contractual consent. Kohlberg's observations on this point are illuminating. He states:

> The social contract which is the basis of the Stage 5 socio-moral order is a justice conception which presupposes reciprocity of the partners to the agreement and equality between them prior to the agreement, though the form of agreement takes priority over substantive justice, once agreement has been reached. Contract and due process are fundamental, and since contracts cannot be binding without the liberty of the contracted, liberty typically takes priority over the other elements of justice (reciprocity and equality) in the Stage 5 view. . .

Shortly afterward he states pointedly:

> Law is nonarbitrary when it accords with constitutional procedures which a rational man could accept without prior cultural values or conditioning. Particular laws are arbitrary, but still binding to a rational man in this context.[6]

At stage 5 there is a heightened awareness of the relativity of the positions held by those in a conflict situation. In the case of the Heinz story cited above, assume that Heinz carried out the theft and is now before the judge. Kohlberg reveals that someone at stage 5 can believe that the husband was morally right in carrying out what appears to be a rational act, stealing the drug to save the life of his wife, while at the same time hold that he was legally wrong and it would be right for the judge to sentence him to jail. The judge must properly discharge his assigned and agreed-upon role even though he, himself, may not think that the husband was morally wrong.

Despite the greater adequacy and universality that characterizes stage 5 structural development in the moral domain, Kohlberg[7] highlights the potential inherent in it for undermining individual rights in favor of the general welfare on some occasions, because of its utilitarian foundation. He chooses as an example an issue of no less significance than that of capital punishment. Stage 5 upholds principles of welfare maximization and of individual rights existing prior to society. In general, both of these principles would be against an essentially retributive punishment. The conflict Kohlberg is leading up to is masked as long as it is believed that there is no evidence to support the deterence theory of execution. In the absence of such evidence there is no gain to the welfare of society's members in capital punishment and hence, in ruling it out, the murder's right to life is preserved. However, assume that compelling documentation to support the deterence theory is submitted. It is now possible to conceive of a situation in which hundreds, perhaps thousands, of lives can be saved yearly by executing apprehended murderers and, of course, running the unavoided risk of occasionally killing an innocent person in error. Kohlberg argues that the utilitarian orientation of maximizing the general welfare would, in the light of evidence supporting deterence, permit a decision in favor of capital punishment. There is nothing in the structural dimensions of stage 5 which allows for a resolution to this potential conflict that could deprive the convicted murderer of his right to life. It is to stage 6 that we must turn to find the completely universalized principles that infuse the highest order of prescriptive moral vision.

### Stage 6: Universal Ethical Principles

The rare person whose sociocognitive moral development has brought him to this stage of moral reasoning is fully autonomous. He is completely decentered from society's expectations and bases his resolutions to ethical conflicts upon universal principles of justice which are prescriptively consistent without exception. Universality, consistency, and logical comprehensiveness are the central attributes that characterize the guiding principles of his conscience through which he chooses right over wrong. Conscience, in this sense, does not connote guilt, but the purely rational quality of his justice structure. Respect for the dignity of each individual, regardless of station in life, has reached a zenith.

Although there is less hard research data on this stage than on any of the preceding ones, Kohlberg devotes more time to exploring it than to all of the others combined. It is here that he may be found at his most philosophical and eloquent. It is also at stage 5 and especially at stage 6 that critics find him most vulnerable. Kohlberg adamently maintains that some ways of resolving moral issues are better than others and it is an absolute that stage 6 moral reasoning offers a better way than any other. It is the highest known stage of moral development and as such offers the most adequate means for arriving at ethical solutions to competing claims between individuals or between individual and the general welfare. The justice principles embraced at this stage lead to ethical resolutions which would be accepted by any rational person who is engaged in moral reasoning uninfluenced by his own existential role and personal interests. The solution itself will be seen as intrinsically and necessarily just, which makes it even more adequate than the justice of stage 5, which comes from consenting to submit to the binding nature of social contract or democratic procedure.

Principled thinking at this stage provides the rationale for breaking the law. At stage 5 there is an emphasis upon working through the democratic process to change an unjust law. Thus, stage 4 appears conservative by comparison. Similarly, to the stage 6 thinker the long change process advocated by the person at stage 5 might seem relatively conservative. At stage 6, an unjust law constitutes sufficient ground for civil disobedience. One's own conscience dictates that compliance with an unjust law is not morally required and that active resistance to it is ethically defensible. An excellent example of stage 6 moral reasoning appeared in the form of a letter to the editor of a large metropolitan newspaper. It was written by Philip Berrigan, the well-known radical priest, and a friend, who were serving six months in prison at the time for protesting nuclear proliferation in the United States. They state that they are questioning the role of the courts and law in America. They then go on to assert, "And we will risk arrest and accept prison because the price of freedom in a society ruled by the Bomb is unconscionably great. The price of freedom is to remain good, law-abiding citizens in the face of preparations for genocide on a scale that will dwarf the holocaust of World War II." Is the stage 6 thinker an anarchist who has no respect for law? An answer comes from a letter by a man in a Birmingham jail. Martin Luther King states, "One who breaks an unjust law must do so openly, lovingly, and with a willingness to accept the penalty. An individual who breaks the law that conscience tells him is unjust, and willingly accepts the penalty of imprisonment in order to arouse the conscience of the community over its injustice is, in reality expressing the highest respect for the law."[8] It is worth noting that an analysis of the public pronouncements of soldiers who followed the command of Lieutenant Calley in the Mai Lai massacre of the Vietnam war reveals that their conception of justice was at stage 4. They believed it was their duty to do as they were ordered to do in this situation. The one soldier who refused to fire has been interviewed privately and Kohlberg has found his explanation for refusing to obey the order to be at a stage 6 principled level of reasoning. This reflects the universality of principles of justice.

There occurs an enlargement across development of the range to which the inherent valuing of human life is extended. At stage 1 we find that value of others' lives is determined by their importance, at stage 3 friends and relatives are those whose lives are essentially valued; by stage 6, however, the inherent value of each person's life and his right to that life are universally recognized. The importance of the person or the moral agent's relationship to him are totally irrelevant as far as an application of the principle is concerned.

We have seen that at stage 5 the morally right is conceived of as contractual and legal. Laws are consensually agreed upon as they are designed to maximize human welfare and promote individual rights. Once legislated, laws should be obeyed, since the citizen has entered a contract, although he may work through the democratic process to have unjust laws changed. At stage 6, an act of civil disobedience is considered an appropriate response to unjust laws because the principles of justice underlying a conception of morality transcend the limitations of the stage 5 utility orientation of maximizing the general welfare of society's members. These principles of justice and a method for arriving at truly just solutions must now be explored.

Kohlberg has offered several excellent philosophical expositions and they have served as major sources for this discussion.[9] A prescriptive right based on principle at stage 6 is one made by a moral agent who has decentered from both his own egoistic impulses and the pressures of others. It therefore becomes a right that is applicable to all individuals. A principle is viewed as a guide to choice which possesses a more abstract quality than a rule. A rule has a more concrete base and cannot be universalized to all people. A rule to be faithful to your spouse cannot be founded upon a universal right that encompasses all people, as clearly not everyone has a spouse. If one were to accept the rule, it still could not apply to children, bachelors, and those who are divorced. A class of acts cannot be universalized, according to Kohlberg, because he believes there is always the possibility that a particular situation might call for a violation of the prescription or proscription involved. Hence, while it might be generally good not to steal, it is morally defensible to steal in the case of the Heinz story, because the wife's right to life takes precedent over the druggist's right to property.[10] Unlike a rule, a principle does not specify the act to be carried out or refrained from. A principle may be construed as a metarule, which is to say that it serves as a higher-order rule or instrumentality for constructing and assessing first-order rules. Cognitively this is rooted in formal operations, where we find the abstract ability to think in terms of second-order propositions as opposed to merely first-order propositions. It is paradoxical that the less abstract conventional-level thinker places the welfare of the more abstract collective above the concrete individual, whereas the more abstract stage 6 moral agent places the rights of the concrete individual in a real situation above the collective's need for order. As Kohlberg states, "From our point of view there is a logical fallacy parallel to elevating the group above its members: the fallacy of treating a principle as elevated above the individuals in the situation to which it applies. . . . True principles guide us to the obligating elements in the situation, to the concrete human claims there."[11] A principle permits the individual to identify and organize, in any specific situation, all moral elements germane to resolving the conflict of competing claims, according to Kohlberg's view.

Kohlberg draws heavily in his formulation of stage 6 thinking upon Kant's two basic moral tenents. One is to always act toward another human being so as to treat him as an end and not merely as a means. The other is to act upon a maxim only if you would be willing to see it embodied as a universal law. By applying the second of these to the first, Kohlberg maintains the outcome is that ". . . all individuals must be accorded fundamentally equal consideration."[12] In his analysis of Kant from which derives the justice principle enunciated in the preceding statement, Kohlberg concludes that treating another as an end and not as means is to be interpreted with respect to rights and claims.

At this juncture in following Kohlberg's argument it is necessary to reintroduce the concept of reversibility, which is a cornerstone to Piaget's genetic epistemology. In fact, he links his particular use of the term to logical thought. There is a mobility of thought in logic which permits shifting from premise to conclusion and back again while averting distortion. Reversibility in the moral domain is isomorphic to the logical domain in relation to rights and duties. Duties and rights have a reciprocal relationship. A right by one person implies a duty by another and, reciprocally, a duty by one implies a right by another. Conversely, in the absence of a right there is no correlative duty. This is an instance of reciprocal implication which is one of the causal relationships comprising the sixteen-binary operational model that governs formal operational thought. Kohlberg amplified his notion of reversibility to add that in the presence of a right others are duty-bound to acknowledge that right. By assuming reversible positions of key individuals in a conflict situation and exercising what Kohlberg calls a second-order conception of Golden Rule role-taking, it is possible for the stage 6 moral agent to arrive at a just and equilibrated ethical solution to conflicts. There exists a state of disequilibrium when competing claims remain unresolved and it is only at stage 6 that a solution which would be satisfactory to all rational individuals, regardless of what role they may find themselves in, may be arrived at. Central to his position is the following clarification by Kohlberg:

> Reversibility of moral judgment is what is ultimately meant by the criterion of the fairness of a moral decision. Procedurally, fairness as impartiality means reversibility in the sense of a decision on which all interested parties could agree insofar as they can consider their own claims impartially, as the just decider would. If we have a reversible solution, we have one that could be reached as right starting from anyone's perspective in the situation, given each person's intent to put himself in the shoes of the other. . . . If something is fair or right to do from the conflicting points of view of all those involved in the situation, it is something we can wish all men to do in all similar situations.[13]

If Heinz is reasoning at stage 6, he will place the druggist in the situation of the dying wife and anticipate whether the druggist would, from that perspective, still hold to the claim of property rights over life. He would then reverse the imaginative drama, have the wife placed in the druggist's situation, and ask whether she would continue to press her claim to life after having experienced that perspective. Kohlberg suggests that the druggist would yield his claim and the wife would not. Once Heinz has undergone this "ideal role-taking," he will see clearly in which direction justice lies. The process described here is what Kohlberg is referring to when he speaks of second-order Golden Rule role-taking. Heinz does not simply put himself in the wife's position but he first imagines himself to be the druggist and then he places himself in the wife's shoes. Thus he takes the perspective of his wife as seen through the eyes of the druggist. This is more complex that the process through which the stage 3 person applies the Golden Rule. At stage 3, if he merely takes the perspective of his wife, then her claim will be valid; if he takes the perspective of the druggist, then his claim will seem valid. Hence, while stage 3 moral reasoning is most assuredly an advance over the preceding stages, it does not offer a fully equilibrated solution to moral conflicts, which is not arrived at until stage 6. It is Kohlberg's conviction that the philosophical analysis he offers is a demonstration of the manner in which justice principles which are universal, consistent, and logically comprehensive are derived.

A *Theory of Justice,* by John Rawls, has made a profound impact since its publication in 1971 and is worthy of comment in connection with Kohlberg's moral system. Rawls's book has already spawned a spate of articles and other books, and it is being speculated that his contribution to political and philosophical thought will be permanent, in the tradition of Plato, Kant, Mills, and Locke. Rawls's analysis of justice focuses upon a level of justice in relation to social institutions and does not have the psychological and individual emphasis which Kohlberg's does. Nevertheless, the central vision of justice as the core structure of morality inextricably links the two thinkers. Rawls has identified two major principles of justice. The first is that each person in society has equal entitlement to maximum liberty that is congenial to a similar liberty for others. The second is related to inequalities within a society regarding social and economic areas. Rawls's contention is that existing inequalities should be only those which are of benefit to everyone. A corollary is that positions of inequality should be affiliated with posts which are equally accessible to all. Injustice for Rawls consists of those inequalities which do not work to the advantage of everyone. Justice is fairness. The principles are to be applied to the entire society, and the second one in particular is concerned with distributive justice, regulating wealth, income, and welfare services, including health and education. The theoretical cornerstone is the idea that citizens are to enter a social contract founded upon principles of justice that all rational people would design and embrace. As a hypothetical device for arriving at justice principles, he offers his notion of imaginatively entering the "original position" under a "veil of ignorance." What he is suggesting is that to design a fair society, one should rationally adopt the perspective of a person who will live in the society after it is conceived, but who at the time of conceiving it does not know anything about what his role in it will be. He remains completely ignorant of the nature of his work and socioeconomic status while he is developing the blueprint. He is to exercise prudence and take into account what the possible effects would be upon him should he find himself in one role or another at a later date. He is to assume that he will, in fact, enter one or more of the roles within the society once it has been designed. In the meantime, he must decide how goods and services are to be distributed and on what basis opportunities are to be made accessible. Rawls believes that all rational people agree upon the justice principles that would be derived through the heuristic device of the original position. He further believes that his own two egalitarian principles, previously stated, may be generated in this manner and that, therefore, all rational people would find them acceptable.

Kohlberg and Elfenbein, in "Capital Punishment," have applied Rawls's device of the original position to the question of whether capital punishment is just. They suggest that no rational person would in advance consent to enter a society that practiced such retributive punishment if there were a chance that he might be a murderer. Yet it would be rational to design some type of deterrence in the penal system, since the hypothetical person might fulfill a role of a noncriminal. It would be prudent to run the risk of facing some restraint as a criminal, should he find himself in that role, to avoid finding himself confronted with criminals on the street, should he turn out to be a noncriminal. Still bearing in mind that he might assume the criminal role, he would favor that deterrence mechanism which places the least constraint upon him while effectively achieving the deterrent goal. Pursuing their analysis through the original position, Kohlberg and Elfenbein conclude that neither capital punishment nor even life imprisonment would be necessary to deter the rational person, as all that would be necessary would be a punishment, ". . . just severe enough to offset the gains which might be realized from the commission of the offense." [14] Their analysis is brought to a close with the following summary statement:

> The judgment that capital punishment per se is unjust is ineluctable if we accept the Stage 6 proposition that the murderer is to be treated as anyone else in his position who also took the roles of others would wish to be treated (as an end rather than a means). As we have stated, the Stage 6 mode of moral reasoning is unique in that it yields a determinate and fully reversible solution. It is therefore the mode we want all men to adopt; if all men did so, they would reach unanimous agreement that the death penalty is morally wrong—on grounds that all who took a moral point of view could accept as fair. [15]

In the context of this discussion, the authors introduce an important theme, which appears to be one about which Kohlberg has a strong conviction. He believes that a social evolution has been occurring which is reflected in a trend toward ultimately stabilizing moral progress at a higher level of development than it has been in the past. The authors express the opinion that this is being applied to retributive forms of justice, which increasingly will be deemphasized in future penal codes in favor of a greater form of justice.

## Stage 7: The Cosmic Perspective

In recent work, "Stages and Aging in Moral Development," and "Education, Moral Development and Faith," Kohlberg has begun introducing the possibility of a seventh stage which assumes a cosmic perspective that goes beyond the humanistic one of the sixth stage. This is a step that moves his theory toward a lifespan developmental psychology, as it would no longer confine itself to the periods of childhood, adolescence, and youth. His speculations on the possibility of this stage are appealing, although he readily acknowledges that there exists no research data to support them presently. Kohlberg suggests that stage 6 does not answer the questions, "Why be moral?" and, by implication, "Why live?" To raise these questions is to shift from a moral plane to a religious or ontological plane. Kohlberg believes that answers to these questions cannot be derived from rational grounds, as with the purely moral issues, but he does feel, nevertheless, that the answers need not be incompatible with reason. Nor need the answer be essentially theistic as opposed to cosmic. Kohlberg speaks of experiencing despair as the beginning of movement into stage 7. The aging person begins to construe his finite life from the infinite perspective of the cosmic, which generates despair, as doubt is cast upon life's meaning, given its temporality. The next phase, however, involves a transition from seeing the infinite perspective to identifying the self with the cosmic perspective of the infinite. A sense of unity with the cosmos imparts a new valuing of one's own life and eliminates the sense of meaninglessness that characterized the preceding phase of despair. In the absence of data, Kohlberg refrains from concluding that what he is elaborating upon signifies a structural advance that would meet the formal criteria, qualifying it as a true stage in the same sense that the preceding stages do. However, whether the cosmic perspective is ultimately determined to qualify as a stage from the standpoint of a structural orientation or not, it is clear that Kohlberg believes spiritual growth is possible among the aging.

## BRIDGING CONVENTIONAL AND POSTCONVENTIONAL MORAL DEVELOPMENT

There are two key papers,[16] dealing with the issues of structural regression and stage transition, which merit special attention within the context of this discussion. The papers are related, as the 1973 one is a revision of the original interpretation made in the 1969 paper of what then appeared to be structural regression. Normally, one would not predict regression from a stage theory as defined by cognitive structuralists, barring such serious developments as senility.

The 1969 paper reports the results of research conducted earlier by Kramer. The subjects were a group of those who were in Kohlberg's own original longitudinal study. They ranged in age from sixteen to twenty-five. Kramer's study was both longitudinal and cross-sectional. The interviewing was conducted at three age levels. A young man in the study would either be compared to his own earlier statements or to those of a boy in another age group. There were a total of forty-five subjects in the study.

One of the conclusions from this study, later to be revised upward, was that stage 5 thinking, when it appeared, was completely stabilized by the time high school had ended. However, it is not until the early twenties that stage 6 thinking, rare though its occurrence may be, is found to be fairly well along in development. On the basis of this data, one would not anticipate that any significant moral development would occur after the early twenties. The stabilization of conventional moral modes of thought after graduation from high school, for those who did not progress to the next moral level, was a significant developmental observation.

The finding that drew the most serious attention was that 20 percent of the middle-class boys slipped from a higher stage to stage 2. Those who did this had ranked among the most developed of the entire group under study. Their previous moral development had reflected a mix of stages 4 and 5. Yet they seemed to retrogress to a stage of hedonistic relativism. Nevertheless, two important qualifications obtained. Even though they were found to be making predominantly stage 2 statements, the content contained a degree of philosophical and political coloration not ordinarily found in stage 2 subjects. Furthermore, when it was explored with them through the clinical interview, the retrogressors displayed an awareness that people generally preferred stage 4 reasoning. Hence, although they seemed to prefer stage 2 reasoning in this regressed condition, they retained a comprehension of stage 4 reasoning. This, of course, would not be true of a person who had arrived developmentally at stage 4 without having regressed. The regression of the subjects had occurred while they were in their senior high school year or early college career. The striking fact is that without exception, by the time they had reached age twenty-five each one had not only been restored to stages 4 and 5 thinking, but there then appeared to be a trifle more of the principled level of moral reasoning than of the conventional, in comparison to when they had been in high school. Sifting through all the pertinent evidence, Kohlberg and Kramer concluded that their subjects had undergone a functional advance although a structural regression. Kohlberg and Kramer, based on an analysis of the subjects' statements, suggest that the regression was a way of coping with guilt from internalized parental authority. Once on the college campus, they attempted to break free of the guilt-inducing constraints. Kohlberg and Kramer comment, as follows:

In the case of our retrogressors, there is considerable use of relativism and antimoral protest to free themselves from familialy induced guilt. At least half of our regressors gave conscious and clear statements of strong sensitivity to and preoccupation with guilt feelings in preadolescence and adolescence. In this preregression period, the guilt was completely accepted as the voice of higher morality, as something self-accepted and internal. At the same time, the capacity of the boy's parents to inflict this sense of guilt was also noted by the boys. After they left home, they started to test out their capacity to be guilt free.[17]

In addition to this psychological phenomenon, the youngsters were being confronted with a challenge to their conventional morality as college life exposed them to the fact that often people did not follow moral precepts or were not rewarded for doing so when they did. Their regression was seen by Kohlberg and Kramer to be partly a rebellion against this realization. The authors go on to observe, "there are, then, two developmental challenges to conventional morality to which our regressors are unhappily responding. The first is the relativity of moral expectations and opinion, the second is the gap between conventional moral expectations and actual moral behavior."[18]

In a liberal adaptation of Erikson's concept of psychological moratorium, Kohlberg and Kramer interpret the retrogressors' condition as a "rebellious moratorium" which frees them from their guilt so that when they are restored to higher-level morality it has more of a volitional quality than a psychically determined one. Return to the higher morality from which they appear to have temporally dropped now has a quality of the "Right thing for the right reason," if I may paraphrase T. S. Eliot. The reaffirmation of the higher stages of morality with its rules and contracts is embraced with greater realism and commitment than prior to regression. The structural regression is also a functional advance in the service of ego development.

I have chosen to treat this issue at considerable length because any true structural regression in normal development would deliver a fatal blow to Kohlberg's invariant sequence and greater adequacy hypotheses. It is also important to pay careful attention to Kohlberg's reworking of any apparent regression for there is always the danger that he may be unwittingly straining at reinterpreting the facts merely to preserve the hypotheses rather than modifying the latter to fit the former, as Brown and Herrnstein incisively caution in *Psychology*. Lastly, the subject we are focusing upon hovers around the transition from conventional to principled moral reasoning, which is a matter of decisive importance.

A span of four years passed before the second paper, which provided more opportunity to explore in depth the developmental changes that the subjects in the longitudinal study were undergoing. Kohlberg and Kramer had claimed that no real structural development was occurring in adulthood and that most of what they observed could be explained in terms of functional stages of the psychosocial variety described by Erikson. However, given new data, a searching conceptual reanalysis of regression in relation to stage theory and a reassessment of the scoring system, a revision was seen to be in order. The change in the scoring system involved a further deemphasis of content, accompanied by a greater attentiveness to structural elements. Essentially, what Kohlberg is now asserting is that the apparent regression of the subjects we have been following is proof that none of their thinking had been morally principled, for if it had been, then it would have been stabilized and would not have yielded to regression in the face of conflict. Genuine stage 5 and stage 6 moral development is crystalyzed in the latter part of one's twenties and beyond.

Kohlberg, drawing upon a conceptual distinction made earlier by Turiel, comments, ". . . the apparent regression involved in stage development is a disequilibrium of transition very different than the disorganization or dedifferentiation involved in regression. . . . our relativistic regressions to Stage 2 are in a disequilibrated transitional stage in which the breakup of conventional morality is easy to confuse with the resurgence of preconventional morality."[19] Kohlberg acknowledges having been in error when he and Kramer interpreted their subjects as having had a structural regression, even though a functional advance. The reinterpretation calls for the identification of a transitional stage to be referred to as stage 4B. What is happening experientially to the subjects is that, having been at stage 4, they start the progression toward stage 5. The movement is characterized by skepticism which leads to a questioning of the very stage they are about to move away from. Their moral reasoning appears relativistic and egoistic, as in stage 2, because they now seem to be holding that any one person's choice, based on his own interests and desires, is as morally sound as another's, as there exists no objectively validated standard against which to assess them. The qualitative difference is that stage 2 children evaluate right and wrong strictly in accord with their personal wish. They lack any concept of a societal perspective or duty. The stage 4 thinker in transition possesses these concepts, but is facing a crisis in that he is challenging—hence his skepticism—the very grounds upon which he had been embracing his conventional morality. He is on the threshold of a breakthrough to principled moral reasoning which, although he does not yet realize it, will supply him with the new standard for which he is striving. In the meantime, he is at neither stage 5 nor stage 2, but has reached a more abstract level of stage 4, which is 4B, than he had been at previously. Kohlberg emphasizes that the stage 4B subject takes a dual relativistic perspective in which he now sees both society's and the personal "selfish" points of view people hold as morally valid.

In "Stage Transition in Moral Development," Turiel views those undergoing the passage from stages 4 to 5 as being temporarily in a state of limbo, having rejected the stability of stage 4 while not yet having invented for themselves the more adequate structure of the stage 5 social contract orientation. What we find characterizing the responses of these stage 4B transitional subjects is a constant vacillation between highly relativistic and rigidly absolutistic solutions to moral dilemmas. This vacillation greatly resembles the cognitive dynamics of a nonconserving child as he moves toward the conservation of substance, first centering upon length and then upon width, but failing to coordinate the two variables in a simultaneous decentering. Similarly, the stage 4B subject who is in transition engages in sequential decentering, alternating between relativism and absolutism, thereby coming up with distorted and inadequate moral solutions. The subject is in transition and experiencing a necessary disequilibrium. Out of this interim phase he forges a new moral vision based upon a social contract structure. The penalty for avoiding the conflict is to remain permanently consigned to a stage 4 version of morality. For those who do go on, Turiel suggests that at some point during the passage to stage 5, "A critical view of Stage 4 absolutism is coupled with an awareness of the relativity of social conventions."[20]

Returning now to Kohlberg, on the basis of the new interpretation he revised his position. Candidly noting the earlier scoring error, he formulates a summary statement, as follows:

We now claim that apparent "retrogression" and "stabilization" was really a structural stage-development, a movement from a high school conventional Stage 4 position to a transitional 4½ ethical relativism and egoism to a principled Stage 5 position. Our earlier interpretation error was due to confusing high school conventional thought with principled thought. We said the confusion was due to the fact that there is an overlap in content between developed forms of conventional concepts of the moral as social consensus and social welfare and principled concepts of the moral. While both the conventional Stage 4B and the Stage 5 orient to socio-moral concerns and welfare, the Stage 5 subject has questioned society's norms but then reaccepted them through the social contract.[21]

Kohlberg revises his comments about the appearance of structural development in adulthood, to acknowledge its actual occurrence. Stage 5 thinking is found to have emerged during the mid-twenties and there were no observed instances of stage 6 moral reasoning in any of the subjects by age thirty. By implication this signifies that stage 6 is a comparatively late development. When one considers that Kohlberg cities such men as Socrates, Jesus, Lincoln, and King as examples of stage 6 morality, its rarity is not surprising, although it has been estimated that 5 percent of American adults achieve this. It only takes a moment's reflection on the fate of the four men identified as examples to raise the intriguing question about the possible inherent danger of being at stage 6 in a predominantly conventional society.

# Chapter Five

# Action, Hierarchy, and Logic

In the preceding chapter the core of Kohlberg's theory of sociomoral knowledge has been presented. It is a theory embedded within a cognitive-developmental framework and built upon Piaget's early work on moral judgment. Although it offers a considerable extension and refinement of Piaget's position, it also departs from that perspective in some important respects. Since the theory's first publication in 1963, Kohlberg's own findings have been subject to an ongoing process of elaboration and refinement. Principal among the participants in this process have been Kohlberg himself, as well as Turiel, Rest, Kuhn, Langer, and Haan, all of whose contributions will be examined below. I have organized this chapter around three major themes, each of which deals with an essential question pertaining to Kohlberg's theory. The first is the relationship between moral development and human action. In Kohlberg's theory, the unit analyzed to determine moral stage is the verbal judgment of the individual, which reflects his conception of justice. However valuable that may be as knowledge for its own sake, many will want to know whether that judgment has any impact in the real world, where people's lives are affected by the way fairness and justice are implemented in interpersonal relationships, bureaucratic organizations, law making, and sometimes in acts of civil disobedience.

The second question has to do with the hierarchical nature of stages and the mechanism which facilitates passage through those stages. What is the relationship of a given stage to those both adjacent and remote from it in the hierarchy? How does the theory account for passage from one stage to the next? To what practical advantage may the answers to these questions be put?

The third and final question to be explored in this chapter is the relationship between logico-mathematical structures as conceived by Piaget and moral development in the Kohlbergian stage theory. Is pure cognitive development sufficient to produce corresponding stages in the moral sphere? If not, is it necessary at all? If it is necessary, but not sufficient, then what might be some of the other variables which perhaps mediate between logico-mathematical mental structures and the justice mental structures?

These questions have been introduced as a preliminary in order to sharpen the focus of the discussion which follows.

## MORAL JUDGMENT AND ACTION

Perhaps the single most important question spurred by the cognitive-developmental approach to sociomoral knowledge is the relationship between type of stage reasoning and behavior. The clear position adopted by proponents of this approach is that stage structure does definitely influence behavior choice. It is acknowledged that variables other than one's stage of moral development will come to bear in determining action. These would certainly include personality attributes, situational conditions, affective arousal, and degree of personal risk or loss involved. Although the cognitive-developmental stage of an individual is, by definition, based on his mode of moral reasoning, which reveals his structural attainment, one could argue that the acid test is the extent to which there is a correspondence between that reasoning and behavior. Certainly we know people are capable of combining lofty pronouncements with base actions. In *The Moral Judgment of the Child,* Piaget pointed to the paradox that sometimes children espouse fidelity to the rule while breaking it at every turn, whereas it may also be observed that at times their behavior is in advance of their moral judgments.

Kohlberg, in "From Is to Ought," believes that confronted with a conflict choice, there is a tendency for a given stage to favor one specific alternative over another, even though it happens that those at different stages may sometimes make the same choice. He holds that individuals at stages 4, 5, and 6 are more likely to be consistent in their behavioral patterns than those in the lower stages. The reason for this is that those at the higher stages are governed by stable considerations based on an objective standard or principle, while those at stages 1, 2, and 3 are governed by more personalized and situational factors, which are more readily subject to change. Principled moral reasoning in particular implies a set of values that have been differentiated and integrated into a hierarchy that is universally shared by people at that level. Therefore, Kohlberg's theory would predict greater consistency and reliability of action among those at the higher level. Behavior itself, however, is not a criterion of the actor's moral developmental level, as it is necessary to know his conception from which the action follows to determine that. For example, one person may march on Washington in a protest against an unjust war. Another may join in the same march because he feels his friends expect it and he would be wrong to go against their wishes. The first is action out of stage 6 principles involving the value of life; the second is behaving out of a conception of right based on group loyalty. The overt behavior of these two people during the day of the march is not demonstrably different, even though their moral conceptions vary vastly and can only be discovered by exploring the meaning the experience has to them. The focus in this section, however, will be upon different behaviors which, from the evidence, seem to be largely influenced by structural development. Kohlberg has pointed out that two individuals at the same stage could very well generate opposite action choices even though the form of their reasoning is the same. For example, one person may compliantly go off to fight a war upon being drafted, on the basis of his stage 4 moral reasoning that the social order can be maintained only if he and all others obey the law of the land and do as they are told by legitimate authority. A second person may become a draft resister based upon the religious dogma of his faith which inveighs against any act of aggression. If his action is predicated upon obedience to religious authority and not a higher principle, then it is as much a form of stage 4 moral reasoning as is the case of one who chooses to go off and fight the war. Nevertheless, as indicated previously, the higher one moves up the developmental scale, the greater the likelihood that the behavioral choice will favor one side of a two-choice conflict, and the lower one moves down the scale, the greater the likelihood that behavioral choice will favor the other side. Kohlberg believes that stage structure imparts a "cognitive disposition" which is the critical element exercised in determining moral action and not the affective element so often emphasized in traditional psychology. Affect itself is neutral with regard to the moral realm. It may or may not be applied to a moral field. When it is, then it may be referred to as moral, but it takes on this character because it has been channeled in that direction by the cognitive disposition which interprets the situation.

The classic study by Hartshorne and May, *Studies in the Nature of Character,* (1928–30), which provided support for the position that honesty is situation-specific, has served as a point of departure for many discussions on the subject over the years. Anticipation of being caught at cheating or not is cited as being a greater determinant of behavior than any hypothetical internal trait of honesty or a unitary notion of conscience. Other factors, such as group pressure and willingness to take a risk, were more significant than a consistent trait of honesty. Kohlberg himself has repeatedly criticized the "bag of virtues" notion of morality as being incorrect. He rejects the idea that there are discrete attributes or virtues, such as honesty, which one either has or does not have. A view of morality based on single isolated virtues is incompatible with a cognitive-developmental position. To that extent, Kohlberg may be said to find the conclusion of Hartshorne and May congenial. However, their research is based on a content analysis of their subjects rather than upon a structural analysis. In "Honesty and Dishonesty," Burton presents a searching exposition of their early work. He highlights that the researchers defined the behaviors studied (i.e., cheating, lying, and stealing) as an active effort at deception. They defined traits as some type of internal disposition which would function independently of the situation. Since they found gross inconsistency in the studied behaviors across situations, they were led to reject the trait theory. Burton argues that Hartshorne and May, however, had some glimmerings of an underlying generality of behavior and that in his own attempts at reanalyzing their original data he found grounds for concluding that, in fact, there was a pattern of resistance to temptations that cut across situations.

Krebs and Kohlberg, in "Moral Judgment and Ego Controls," have reported research substantiating the view that certain internal variables are predictive of moral behavior and, contrary to Hartshorne and May's conclusion, that moral behavior is not essentially determined by situationally related dynamics. This may be qualified by indicating that the degree to which situational determinants are paramount is a function of moral level. Kohlberg and Krebs hold that the forces operating within a situation are most likely to affect the person at a preconventional level. At the conventional level there exists more of a dual pull or battle between the forces in the situation and a person's moral stage development. The struggle is mediated by the "moral will," which in this study is construed as ego controls constituted by attentional stability. The person at the principled level is not influenced by situational forces and does not undergo a struggle of conscience, as his course is determined by rational considerations derived from principles. Before presenting some of the pertinent data and discussion, it is necessary to make one further qualifying comment. Kohlberg and Krebs are applying their analysis to what is referred to as minor moral decision making. It is the absence of intense sacrifice that defines that task as minor. In the event that intense sacrifice is a variable, then even for adults at the principled level, it may be necessary to reintroduce ego controls to steadfastly hold to the correct moral action as dictated by rational reflection at the principled level. Although this is a vital distinction, it does not mitigate the value of the material presented below, when its limitations are understood.

The study reported by Kohlberg and Krebs had a population of 123 sixth-grade subjects, ranging from lower class to upper middle class. Sex and social class variables were balanced. Mean IQ was always above 107, whether viewed by sex or social class. Children in the study were tested for resistance to temptation, cheating behavior, attentional stability, and moral stage.

The results clearly indicated that moral judgment was predictive of the subjects' actual behavior in situations designed to tempt them to engage in cheating. It was found that among stage 5 subjects 80 percent resisted cheating, and among stage 4 subjects 45 percent resisted cheating. In sharp contrast, from a combined count of those in stages 1, 2, and 3, only 25 percent resisted cheating. Taking stage 1 separately, only 19 percent resisted. A factor of further interest to the researchers was whether attentional ability was related to resistance and how this variable interacted with moral stage. They equated attentional processes with the notion of William James that the capacity to attend an object through an act of volitional effort constitutes moral will. However, attentional stability is not intrinsically a moral factor in the Kohlbergian sense, as it is clearly applicable to both moral and nonmoral tasks alike. The major discovery was that the variable of attentional stability, construed as ego control, had a differential effect related to moral stage. Attention was found to have a significant effect upon stage 4 thinkers, increasing the likelihood that subjects at that stage would resist the temptation to cheat. The data revealed that of high-attending stage 4 subjects, 56 percent refrained from cheating, whereas of low-attending stage 4 subjects only 33 percent did so. In contrast, it was found that high attention was associated at the preconventional level with increased cheating. This was especially true at stage 2, where the data reflect that while 75 percent of the low-attending refrained from cheating, the high-attending subjects who resisted came to 20 percent only. Hence, we find a reversal of effect of high attention when we go from stage 4 to stage 2. Kohlberg and Krebs point out that lower-stage morality by its very nature is more situation-specific. In explaining the ostensibly surprising effect of high ego control being associated with low resistance to cheating at lower moral stages, they state:

> The pre-conventional child is determined in his moral reasoning by the immediate situation. Ego factors, then, support the child's reasoning and choice, but this reasoning and choice is not consistently moral. For the lower stage child moral judgment is not a force independent of, or opposed to, the situation. Accordingly ego factors do not oppose situational pressures or temptations for the lower stage child. For the lower stage child, ego factors of attention and brightness aid the child to "do well" in a task as "doing well" is defined by social situational forces. "Doing well" for a lower stage child, however, is more likely to mean cheating to gain a reward or a "good score" than it is to mean displaying "moral strength."[1]

It follows, Kohlberg and Krebs reason, that when the low attending preconventional subjects abandon their task from distractibility, the task they are abandoning is cheating, which their structural level of moral development permits them to engage in as right in certain situations. Consider the following observation by Kohlberg and Krebs, which contains a comparative statement, as follows:

> The lower stage subject is just as likely as the higher stage subject to judge cheating as bad or wrong on attitude scales. The "wrongness" of cheating for lower stage subjects, however, is interpreted in terms of, or

incontingency upon, situational forces of punishment, reward, authority, and group status which can, under certain conditions, predispose toward cheating as much as predisposing against it. At higher stages, the "wrongness" of cheating is defined in terms of considerations of trust and equity which predispose against cheating regardless of most situational forces.[2]

It is reported that five principled subjects (80 percent) resisted the temptation. These were all at stage 5 and interestingly they measured as low-attending. Because of the felicitous separation between the variables of attentional ability and moral stage, it is clear that high moral stage in itself is sufficient to produce moral behavior based on principle. As for preconventional children who do not cheat, Kohlberg and Krebs do not view them as having faced an internal struggle of conscience, mediated by ego controls with a victory for moral behavior. They are simply not tempted to cheat because of their definition of the situation. For example, a stage 1 child who anticipates a decisive penalty for violating a rule is simply less likely to be tempted to cheat. In the final analysis, it is the stage 4 subject who faces the internal struggle in the face of genuine temptation. It is at this stage that ego controls as a mediating variable play a most crucial role in assisting the youngster toward the choice to resist temptation. The stage 4 person is committed to a conception of right that entails following the rules promulgated by society as a general abstraction. Hence, in a situation designed to tempt him to cheat, he enters a state of conflict between situational pressures and moral stage dictates. The exceptional situation had been set up in such a way that the immediate pressure was toward cheating because of the opportunity afforded to do so. Lacking a set of universally consistent principles, the stage 4 person becomes conflicted. It is at this stage that moral will power, construed in terms of high level attentional processes, becomes decisive in assisting the subject to resist temptation.

Kohlberg in "From Is to Ought," cites similar research conducted by Brown et. al., who carried out their work with undergraduates, and described it in "Some Correlates of Conflict." Half of the conventional-level subjects cheated, while out of nine postconventional students only one cheated. Kohlberg concludes:

A Stage 5 or 6 person defines the issue as one of maintaining an implicit social contract with the tester and others taking the test. The more unsupervised, the more trusting the experimenter, the more contractually obligated this principled person is. Also, the principled person defines the issue of cheating as one of inequality, of taking advantage of others, of deceptively obtaining unequal opportunity, that is, in terms of justice. . . . This interpretation implies *that moral judgment determines action by way of concrete definitions of rights and duties in a situation.*[3]

It would seem that while Hartshorne and May were perhaps on solid ground in rejecting a simplistic notion of an all-or-none honesty trait that imparts consistency across all situations, they were incorrect to give little credence to an internal disposition that influences moral behavior independently of situational forces. Although possessed by few, principled cognitive-structural reasoning would seem to qualify as just such an internal variable. Furthermore, ego control, defined as volitional attention, when exercised by the stage 4 person, also qualifies as an internal variable that influences the actor toward a moral choice of honesty. These developmental phenomena are obviously more complex than the single-trait theory, but there is evidence to support Kohlberg's interpretation of their role in moral behavior.

While the above research of Krebs and Kohlberg focuses upon young children in minor decision making, the classic findings of Haan, Smith, and Block, in "Moral Reasoning of Young Adults," shift our attention to young adults in a critical situation. Whereas subjects in the former were acting under contrived laboratory conditions, those in the latter acted spontaneously in their natural environment. The subjects consisted of students from the University of California at Berkeley and from San Francisco State College, and of a group of Peace Corps volunteers in training. A total of 957 respondents, chosen at random from the registration files, responded by completing five of the moral dilemma stories devised by Kohlberg. Of that group, 54 percent were chosen for the study because, on the basis of very stringent criteria, they could be scored as being in a pure stage without ambiguity. Assignment to a pure type signified that they had at least twice the score at that stage than at any other stage, across all five stories, as assessed by two judges. The subjects also filled out an extensive questionnaire providing biographical information, and took some additional tests regarding child rearing and self-concepts. The self-concepts identified pertained to both perceived self and ideal self.

Students in the study were enrolled in their educational activities in 1964, at the time of the famous Berkeley student revolt, which revolved around the Free Speech movement. Administrative officials restricted political activity by students on the Berkeley campus and many students, as well as other activists, protested on campus by acting in violation of the prohibitions. A major sit-in, occurring in December 1964, led to many arrests by the police. A subsection of the present research analyzes by moral types those student activists who were arrested. We shall return to the smaller sample of those students arrested at Berkeley in 1964 after noting some distinctive features of the larger sample of students from both universities and the Peace Corps volunteers.

Subjects at the principled level of morality were more radical politically and tended to strongly favor the Free Speech movement. There was a greater incidence among them of having interrupted their college career and of living apart from the campus in apartments or houses. They described themselves more frequently as being atheistic, agnostic, or areligious. Their parents were seen by them as liberal in politics. The principled subjects had been comparatively more active in sociopolitical affairs and had a background of involvement in organizations and protest activities. It was found that the ideal self of principled men was a perceptive, empathic, and altruistic one. They specifically disavowed the trait of stubbornness and emphasized the value of self-expressiveness. The researchers observe that this configuration of attributes implicitly espouses role-taking virtues, which are essential to high moral development in the Kohlbergian scale. The principled women described themselves as being altruistic, but dissatisfied for having feelings of guilt and doubt and being both restless and impulsive. In general, the principled young adults rejected conventional mores and seemed more autonomous than the others. They appeared to place a high value on interpersonal sensitivity and responsibility, as well as self-expressiveness and candor. Based upon their data, the researchers, two of whom are women, suggest that women might have a more difficult time achieving moral and ego autonomy by the time of young adulthood than do men. They indicate further that this may be because there is a clash between autonomous attributes and the stereotyped feminine roles that women had been locked into. In this connection, it is noteworthy that Gilligan has recently advanced a revised and differentiated construction of moral development in "In a Different Voice," specifically based upon women's experiences.

The conventional subjects were the most conservative of the three moral levels, as was true of their parents. They had few instances of interruption in their college careers, tended with greater frequency to live on campus, and had the most religious background and affiliations. The idealized self-concept they cited embodied an emphasis upon social skills and self-control. The men in particular valued order, competitiveness, and ambition, and appeared to shun the very attributes embraced in the idealized self-concept of their principled counterparts. Hence, they devalued self-expressiveness and interpersonal responsiveness. The women held to a similar conception of the ideal, although of special interest is that their version of an ideal self-concept included the apparently contradictory traits of competitiveness and self-denial. Attributes of sensitivity and rebelliousness were not highly regarded by them, just as these were not by conventional men. In general, the conventional subjects were raised in families and communities in which they were exposed to greater harmony and clearer expectations of traditional rules to be followed. They were exposed to less skepticism and conflict than the principled subjects had been. They seemed to have followed the examples of their conservative parents, whereas the principled subjects appeared to possess greater freedom to diverge from the thinking and ideologies of their liberal parents.

The preconventional group contained no stage 1 subjects. The stage 2 subjects comprising it were referred to as Instrumental Relativists. These young people had a comparatively high incidence of interrupted college careers, greater than the case with either principled or conventional youth. The men viewed themselves as radicals or liberals and the women had a perception of themselves as moderate liberals. The men, although not the women, had the highest incidence of off-campus living. Political differences between the male youths and their fathers were greatest in this class. In striking contrast the females within this group shared complete congruence with their mothers on political issues. The women belonged to many organizations, but were relatively inactive compared to the men, who joined fewer organizations, but engaged more intensely in the activities involved. In general, the men were extremely active in political protest and assumed a strongly radical posture. They evidenced greater paternal conflict and anger than any of the other subjects. Although they embraced a self-concept of being reserved and not particularly responsive interpersonally, they saw themselves as highly individualistic and also creative. Among all other subjects they devalued altruism. Their ideal self-concept possessed attributes of stubbornness, detachment, and unyieldingness to compromise solutions and yet it also included spontaneity and artistic ability. Women in this group did not seem to value personal expressiveness to the extent that the men did, but instead emphasized pursuing and attaining personal goals. They idealized practicality and stubbornness. At the same time they placed a high value on becoming idealistic and sensitive. The general picture for both young men and women at this preconventional level reflected an absence of a sense of interpersonal responsibility and a strong commitment to achieving self-fulfillment. They seemed to have had an upbringing characterized by parental indulgence based upon the parents' own convenience and interest. Haan et al. suggest that such rearing fosters unpredictability and mitigates mature moral development because it fails to introduce clear communications about reciprocal rights and duties.

Haan et al. see a striking contrast between the Instrumental Relativists, stage 2, and the Individual Principled subjects, stage 6. The comparative evaluation made by the researchers is worth citing:

> The two groups differ in their relationship to society and to authority. The IPs are independent and critical, but also involved, giving and responsive to others. The IRs are angry, also critical, but disjointed, uncommitted to others, and potentially narcissistic. It should not be surprising to find moral heterogeneity among protestees. Protest which opts for change and accommodation in the social order should draw support from individuals who question the justice of the status quo and are committed to improving it, as well as from those who want to win an issue simply because it is theirs.[4]

The moral stage development of subjects from the University of California has been fruitfully examined in relation to whether they were arrested while participating in the Free Speech movement on the Berkeley campus in 1964. Through such an examination it is possible to derive information on the relationship between behavior and conceptions of morality. It is important to take cognizance of the emphasis by Haan et al. upon the fact that the actual sit-in protest during which the students were arrested was preceded by months of public debate among the students and conflict with the administration. Therefore, participation in the protest is not likely to have been impulsive or the result of a bandwagon effect, but more probably the outcome of a carefully considered decision.

Inspection of the findings supports Kohlberg's contention that moral stage of development bears a relationship to human action. Stages 3 and 4, the conventional level, account for the lowest number of arrests. Of the total population of University of California male students at stage 4, only 6 percent were arrested and of those at stage 3 only 18 percent. Contrasted to this, it was found that 75 percent of the stage 6 and 41 percent of the stage 5 male students were arrested. The difference is striking. What is of especial significance beyond this, however, is that 60 percent of the male students at stage 2 were also arrested. The importance of being arrested in this study is, of course, that only those who were engaged in prominent activist roles were likely to have been picked up by the police. On the basis of the moral conceptions undergirding each stage one would predict low involvement for conventional thinkers and high involvement for principled ones. This is exactly what the survey reflects. However, it might be instructive to ask why any of the conventional level subjects participated at all. Haan et al. had added a story situation revolving around the Free Speech movement to the five Kohlberg stories and that additional story had been specifically administered to the Berkeley students. The responses of the stage 4 arrested students revealed their belief that the authorities had not maintained proper legal procedures in inhibiting the right of free speech. The stage 3 students who were arrested also believed that the authorities had defaulted in their role, but the emphasis for these students was upon the authorities failing to be "good" people. The stage 2 students expressed concern about the repression of their own rights and construed the situation as a power conflict. Lastly, the principled subjects were primarily concerned with the breach of community and citizens' rights represented by the conflict. Thus, an analysis in each case reveals that although those arrested cut across the spectrum of stages, the meaning to the individual actor was determined by the stage of moral development he had reached. The stage 4 subjects who were protesting did not behave, for example, as would be predicted, but an understanding of their moral reasoning reveals a structural conception of justice consistent with stage 4 thinking. This serves to highlight the strong phenomenological cast to Kohlberg's model of moral stages. It also emphasizes that behavior alone is not sufficient for a judgment on the morality of the actor. It is necessary to know the underlying conception of right and wrong that generates the behavior. As long as conventional-level moral reasoners believe that authorities are acting properly, they are not likely to challenge the prevailing status quo, but will embrace it and exhibit compliance. Regarding the stage 2 thinker, Haan et al. point out that since he does not engage in mature role-taking skills, he is likely to protest merely on the basis of frustration of his own wishes. The principled thinker, in contrast has differentiated self from subjective wish and the social perspective, having become free to engage in moral reasoning that is universal, consistent, and objective. He engages in a form of role-taking which entails placing himself at the other person's perspective to understand that viewpoint and reciprocally inquiring how he might want the other to act on his behalf when he is deprived of his own rights. The inference is that the subject should act on another's behalf as he would want the other to act for him. Only about 20 percent of the total subjects at stage 6 did not get arrested, whereas about 50 percent of the stage 5 subjects did and 50 percent did not. Brown and Herrnstein offer a cogent explanation of this even split in *Psychology* by underscoring the social contract nature of the moral reasoning involved at this stage, which lends itself to a more probable even split than in the case of the more fully principled subjects at stage 6 or the egoistic ones at stage 2. Clearly, sitting in could be justified on the grounds that although it violates the law that had been laid down, there were transcendent principles involved. These subjects were already adjacent to a more fully principled level of ethical thinking in their present stage and so it is not surprising that they would move in that direction. However, the structure of their present stage reasoning calls for full utilization of available legal change mechanisms. The university did provide such procedures for instituting change of existing policies and, therefore, it would be expected that many stage 5 students would opt to use them rather than engage in civil disobedience. Of significance in our analysis is the fact that stage 5 students who did not sit in and both stage 5 and stage 6 students who did sit in, shared a more common value base than did stage 5 and 6 protesters in comparison to stage 2 protesters.

In "Hypothetical and Actual Moral Reasoning," Haan compared the stage reasoning of the Berkeley students as scored from hypothetical Kohlbergian moral dilemmas and the stage of moral reasoning used by them in explaining their own actual behavior in relation to the Free Speech movement sit-in which resulted in so many arrests. Her formulation, as well as the empirical findings, encompassed three categories. Altogether two-thirds of the students explaining their actions used a stage different from the moral stage score they had received for reasoning in hypothetical situations. It was found that 46 percent invoked a higher stage and 20 percent a lower stage. Hence, moral reasoning used to explain behavior in an actual situation was either higher, lower, or the same in relation to that utilized in hypothetical situations. Haan's view was that the same reasoning could be accounted for by a subject having fully stabilized his moral development stage. Students who had already begun to show evidence of reasoning at the next stage, hence were already moving in that direction, were likely to be those who would show a gain in stage reasoning. She points out that the leaders of the Free Speech movement were presenting arguments publicly, over a period of time, which were at higher stages than the majority of the students. This could produce the conflict and disequilibrium necessary for stage transition. Finally, personal factors in the pressured situation which the Berkeley student revolt certainly induced could account for loss in stage reasoning in actual behavior for some students due to disorganization. This need not be viewed as moral regression because of the complex nature of the situation. It may be analogous to a child performing nonegocentrically at a simple task, but egocentrically at a complex task. The underlying structure or competence has not been altered in such a situation, but performance is influenced by task or situational complexity. The stage 4 students tended not to show any marked split between reasoning pertaining to the actual situation and that applied to the hypothetical stories. In other words, they essentially reasoned the same in both situations. Those at the principled level demonstrated a fairly even division between students who maintained their stage of reasoning and those who fell below their stage when going from hypothetical to actual circumstances. The tendency on the part of those at stage 2 and 3 was toward moving from a lower to higher stage. Haan has addressed specifically those students who favored the Free Speech movement, but did not participate in the sit-in and who lost a stage in going from reasoning in the hypothetical situation to the actual one. She suggests that these students suffered a sense of inconsistency and diminished integrity because they did not sit in. As a result, in reflecting upon their actual behavior, there occurred some disorganization as they attempted to justify or rationalize the apparent incongruity between not participating in the protest while favoring the cause. The evidence from this study supported the contention that gains were most frequently found among the developmentally ready. One sign of this readiness was the fact that those who gained had already exhibited a greater frequency of use of reasoning at one stage above their scored stage than those who did not gain. This would make them more susceptible to influence by leaders speaking at a higher level, as research to be examined later will testify. There was also biographical data indicating that the gain group was more challenging and skeptical in relation to authority by comparison to the loss group, whose members were more interpersonally bound to their parents. Haan chooses to place emphasis upon action itself as the critical factor, in experientially profound situations, accounting for stage growth. In contemplating the statement below, bear in mind that the Berkeley subjects, while reasoning about their own actions, had done so after the actions had been engaged in, in order to provide data for the study. We do not know what their thoughts were prior to their actions. Haan comments:

> We see then that the theory's normative, genetic description of gain is approximately correct, that mere confrontation with moral conflict is sufficient to enable most university students of lower stages to use higher stage forms, and that action that is consistent with ideology apparently energizes moral thought. When the action is nontrivial, it may well be the first, rather than the last manifestation of an evolving comprehension of more sufficient moral structuring than can yet be articulated in a cognitive-hypothetical way. Nevertheless, it can readily be observed in moral interviews that hypothetical decision is not a pallid experience, since people struggle with the elegance of their suppositional resolutions. Still, moral action is not required, and therein lies the rub: Action actualizes, while thoughts can always be taken back. Moral situations of less consequence and duration probably produce more equivalence and less change.[5]

The above statement by Haan has been quoted at length because of the central role which it assigns to action, as being instrumental in inducing moral stage growth when the subject is in a state of readiness. This emphasis is crucial and different from the customary one of action flowing from the present stage.

Sameness or equality of reasoning between hypothetical and actual conditions was generally typified by those whose moral stage structure and ideological commitment were consistent with one another and with the behavior they engaged in. For example, a stage 6 thinker who interpreted the situation as one obliging him to act out of principle to protect individual rights, favor the Free Speech movement, and participate in the sit-in, had no impetus to shift from reasoning about the hypothetical to actual conditions. This is in contrast to the stage 6 person mentioned previously who favored the Free Speech movement, but did not actively protest, an inconsistency which could lead to rationalization.

The loss groups were, in fact, comprised mainly of those who did not sit in. They were largely stage 5 and a few stage 6 students. Also included in this group were ideologically uncommitted stage 4 students. Haan believes that the cause of their going from a higher to lower form of reasoning is less likely to be found in the moral realm than the socio-affective arena. This is largely based on the biographical data reflecting conflict with authority around obedience and disobedience.

Haan's research and speculation perhaps make their greatest contribution by alerting the moral cognitive-developmental student to the complexity and diversity of considerations to be taken into account when thinking about the relationship between moral stage and human action.

Because of the potentially devastating implications, one of the most significant findings in the field of moral development and behavior is a spin-off of research originally conducted by Milgram and described in *Obedience to Authority*. The experiment was ostensibly an attempt to observe the effect of punishment upon learning by a person who was given tasks to perform and who was to receive shocks from the volunteer subjects whenever he made a mistake. The intensity of the shock was seemingly modulated and beyond 75 volts the learner, who in actuality was a collaborator of the experimenter, would convincingly pretend to be in great pain. The deceived volunteers did not know that real shocks were not, in fact, being administered. Subject to encouragement and pressure from the experimenter to continue increasing the intensity of the shocks, despite escalating cries of agony from the learner, the volunteers could be observed undergoing unmistakably great stress. However, when volunteers would hesitate, the experimenter would escalate the commanding quality of his pressure to continue, going so far as to say, "You have no choice, you *must* go on." The experiment has been replicated in a variety of ways. The essential finding that has impressed Milgram is the extreme length to which otherwise perfectly decent people will go upon the command of an accepted authority, even at the expense of inflicting great pain upon another, as the volunteer subjects truly thought they were doing. It was clear that they believed they were acting wrongly and that they, too, were suffering as they increased the voltage along the scale from 15 to 450. In the original experiment, which was conducted at Yale University, the full voltage was administered by 65 percent of the volunteer subjects. In "Indoctrination Versus Relativity," Kohlberg scored the moral stage of one group of undergraduates who participated in this experiment. The results have not been published in detail, but Kohlberg reports in passing that 75 percent of stage 6 subjects terminated the experiment rather than persist, despite the commands, in causing pain to another. All volunteers below stage 6 continued with the shocks to an extensive degree except for 13 percent, who terminated early in the experiment. This group included the stage 5 moral reasoners, which might appear surprising to some. Kohlberg suggests that stage 5 social contract thinking does not provide adequate principles for resolving the dilemma. The individual has entered into an agreement with the experimenter and the learner has also consented to participate. There exists an obligation to meet one's commitments. It is only the autonomous stage 6 thinker whose principled reasoning transcends the bonds of the social contract to reject the experimenter's authority to command him. As Milgram agrees, the implications are frightening. One has only to recall the Nazi era or the Mai Lai incident to be reminded of the cruelty and destruction that can come through obedience to authority. A point to be reemphasized is that the total group of people who participated in the set of Milgram experiments were decent individuals from all walks of life. Many were dismayed afterward at their own conduct and had to be debriefed to alleviate some of the distressed feelings they were experiencing.

Observing that the research has tended to highlight the behavior of moral reasoners at the principled level as compared to the conven-

tional, Krebs and Rosenwald deliberately executed research that focused exclusively upon examining the relationship between behavior
and moral structural development of the average person at stages 3
and 4, as discussed in their "Moral Reasoning and Moral Behavior."
The subjects were volunteers who answered a newspaper ad offering
them three dollars to participate in a psychological testing experiment. There were thirty-one of them from diversified backgrounds.
Ages ranged from seventeen to fifty-four, with twenty-three years
being the mean. It is especially important to explicate the procedure
in this experiment for full appreciation of what took place and the
results. The subjects assembled in a lecture hall. They were told that
the time desired for the testing was an hour and a half, but that as it
turned out they would only have one hour for the hall, unexpectedly.
The person leading the group identified herself as an undergraduate
student who was conducting the present project for data needed to
complete requirements for a course. It would be necessary for her to
have the test and personality questionnaire in her hands within seven
days or her grade for the course would be endangered. In view of the
shortened time allotted them, she explained that they would be asked
to do only part of the required tasks in the lecture hall and that they
would be issued the necessary materials involved in the balance of
the tasks. Provided with a self-addressed stamped envelope and the
questionnaire to take home, they were strongly urged to complete the
form and mail it back within a week. Before leaving they were paid
the three dollars, the leader emphasizing that she would trust them
not to let her down. During the one hour in the lecture hall they took
the Kohlberg moral development test and supplied biographical data.

An analysis of the scores on the Kohlberg test indicated that 83
percent of the subjects were at the conventional level. Altogether,
despite the great emphasis on the importance of having the questionnaire back on time to avoid jeopardizing the leader's grade, 39 percent of the participants did not return them within the week. Of that
group, 23 percent never returned the questionnaires and 16 percent
managed to get them in, but after the deadline. The completed forms
of all stage 4 and 5 participants were promptly returned and in the
hands of the leader within the time frame requested, with one exception. Among stage 3 subjects, 40 percent were on time, 33 percent
were late, and 27 percent did not return their questionnaires at all.
There were only three stage 2 subjects in the population. One of

them returned the questionnaire on time and the other two did not return them at all. All of the questionnaires that were returned late came from Stage 3 subjects. In brief, the higher the stage, the more likely that the questionnaires would be returned; the lower the stage, the less likely that they would be returned.

Utilizing the biographical data that had been obtained on the day the subjects were all present in the lecture hall, Krebs and Rosenwald were able to rule out such variables as education, sex, and social class as having any significant bearing. Engaging in what they refer to as a clinical analysis, Krebs and Rosenwald concluded that, in fact, it is the moral reasoning, as tested by Kohlberg's dilemmas, which governed the behavior of the subjects. Their clinical analysis is essentially that of noting the logic of correspondence between a subject's moral stage and his behavior in the experiment. Once the three dollars had been received and the relationship terminated, there was nothing to be gained by bothering to return the completed questionnaires, just as there was nothing to be lost by not returning them. Since there was no reward for sending the forms back and no punishment for failing to do so, two of the three instrumental hedonists of stage 2 did not fulfill the contract. There exists the possibility that the one who did return the questionnaires might actually have been at stage 4B, in the light of Kohlberg's revised scoring system. However, this is not known.

Krebs and Rosenwald compare the moral reasoning of their stage 3 subjects to those in stage 4 in order to account for the observed differences in behavior. The central distinguishing factor seemed to be that stage 3 subjects conceived of interpersonal commitments as depending upon knowing someone as a friend, whereas they did not acknowledge moral obligations to strangers. In contrast, the responses in the Kohlberg test revealed that the stage 4 subjects recognized a binding commitment in terms of social rules. Adhering to social norms is necessary among all people if order is to be maintained. Although there is reason to believe that stage 3 subjects are susceptible to group pressure, once having left the experimental setting they were no longer exposed to any external influences toward conformity. Hence, it is consistent with this analysis to discover that out of fifteen stage 3 subjects, a total of nine did not return their questionnaires on time. Of those nine, there were five who eventually turned them in late, while the remaining four never turned them in at all. Krebs and

Rosenwald interpret the fact that five of the nine did turn the questionnaires in late and that no other stage group was in the late category, as suggestive of the indecision characterizing this population when the structural stage of its members is translated into behavior. The researchers assume these subjects knew it was right to meet the obligations inherent in the informal agreement that they had made, yet they had not reached a plane of consistently integrating structure and action. Their emphasis upon personal familiarity and the lack of external group pressure mitigate fulfilling obligations that they had contracted for. In the absence of such mitigating factors and in the presence of structural reasoning that honors rules and the maintaining of social order, it is not at all surprising to find that out of eleven stage 4 subjects, ten returned their questionnaires on time. There was one subject out of the eleven who never returned his questionnaire. None of the eleven returned the questionnaire late. Of course, the fact that the two stage 5 subjects returned their questionnaires and did so on time hardly needs commenting upon at this point, given the greater adequacy of the principled reasoning which characterizes the quality of their moral structure.

Krebs and Rosenwald believe that it is precisely the type of low-pressure situation, with opportunity for reflection, which they simulated, that affords the soundest predictive grounds from Kohlberg's stages. They caution that crisis situations entailing impulsive, nonreflective behavior would not lend themselves as readily to predictions of high reliability. The relationship between moral stage and action depends upon time for cognitive-structural mediation. The type of situation for which they believe Kohlberg's test has the most predictive power is of a more commonplace everyday variety than those involving emergencies and heroics.

## HIERARCHY AND TRANSITION
## IN MORAL GROWTH

Piaget, with a smile passing over his lips, has frequently called the question of whether cognitive development can be hastened, "The American Question." He does so because whenever he lectures in the United States the inquiry is invariably made. The position he has adopted is that given a normal amount of environmental opportunity, the child will properly interact with his milieu and construct the necessary structures for adaptation. Piaget points out that cats reach the significant stage 4 in object permanence more quickly than the human infant, but unlike the latter a cat does not continue past that stage in the cognitive hierarchy to representational thought and the acqusition of language. Therefore, the pace of growth may not be nearly as important as the process and outcome. The fact remains that only about 50 percent of the population appears to acquire fully developed formal operations. Even more conservatively, it has been estimated that only from 10 percent to 20 percent of the population reach the principled level of moral reasoning. Although stage 4 of the conventional level is where most people seem to be, it is still a limited form of morality from the standpoint of justice. Once one accepts justice as the core of morality, as Kohlberg does, then the issue of facilitating movement in the individual through the hierarchy of moral stages can hardly be seen as a trivial matter. Indeed, Kohlberg has engaged in extensive programs designed to acclerate moral growth among those in such diverse institutional settings as public schools and prisons.

Anyone who has followed this study from the beginning will surely realize that Kohlberg's approach to stimulating advance toward moral maturity will not consist of attempting to inculcate character traits such as honesty, courage, or cooperation. This would be tantamount to the Aristotelian "bag of virtues" method which Kohlberg dismisses as antithetical to cognitive-structural theory. Nor would it be anticipated that the trainer would simply attempt to teach a higher stage to the subject in any mechanistic or content oriented fashion. First of all, we know that the individual cannot leap over a stage, so clearly the focus is relative in that it must be upon the stage one step beyond his present predominant stage. Equally significant, is that the individual, interacting with the environment, must construct for himself the qualitative advance inherent in what is for him the next stage. He cannot be taught the stage by someone simply transmitting information about it to him. The equilibration model proffered by Piaget to explain cognitive development generally, also has great utility when applied to explaining moral stage advance. The dynamic of the model may be harnessed and consciously channeled into a social or experimental setting to facilitate moral growth. Turiel, in an excellent resource on stage transition, has stated succinctly:

There are two interrelated aspects to the principle of equilibration. The first refers to equilibrium within structures that form coherent wholes: stages are defined as organized ways of thinking and relating to events. The second refers to equilibrium in the interaction of the individual with the environment. Stages in a developmental sequence are, then, successive levels of equilibrium in two respects. First, each stage is a more equilibrated form than the previous ones (e.g., there is more internal consistency). Second, each stage represents a more equilibrated means of interacting with the environment. That is, each new stage is a more adequate way of understanding moral problems and resolving conflicts encountered.[6]

Central to moving from one stage to the next is the experiencing of conflict induced by encountering events that one's present stage of development cannot adequately encompass or resolve. The very organization of the milieu one is in may be more or less conducive to inducing the disequilibrium necessary for growth. For example, a youth who moves away from home to attend college may be leaving behind an orderly and stable intellectual existence which he had been experiencing in a community of rarely challenged homogenous values. Upon stepping onto the college campus, he finds himself surrounded by a diversity of viewpoints and backgrounds. Challenge and skepticism become the order of the day. Only the most rigid and insulated of students could escape the inevitable conflict and accompanying development. It is perhaps too often overlooked that the primary contribution of college is not the imparting of information, but the promotion of an equilibrating process that cuts across all disciplines, bringing the student forward to a new perspective for understanding and functioning within his sociomoral world. It is in this sense, of undergoing genuine development, that one truly cannot go home again, to borrow a phrase from Thomas Wolfe. In one of his frequent more philosophical moods, Kohlberg has commented upon the role of conflict thusly:

> The first stage in teaching virtue, then, is the Socratic step of creating dissatisfaction in the student about his present knowledge of the good. This we do experimentally by exposing the student to moral conflict situations for which his principles have no ready solution. Second, we expose him to disagreement and argument about these situations with his peers. Our Platonic view holds that if we inspire cognitive conflict in the student and point the way to the next step up the divided line, he will tend to see things previously invisible to him.[7]

Turiel, in "An Experimental Test," has taken the lead in explicating and researching the area of stage transition through cognitive conflict in the field of sociomoral knowledge. Based upon cognitive-developmental theory, Turiel tested two hypotheses. The first was that subjects would manifest greater change in stage status upon having been exposed to reasoning that is one stage above their dominant stage than would other subjects who had been exposed to reasoning that was two stages above their dominant stage. The rationale was that, given the invariant sequence hypothesis of Kohlberg, the assimilation of new moral concepts would be limited by the subjects' present stage. The second hypothesis tested by Turiel was that subjects exposed to one stage above their present one would exhibit more stage gain than those exposed to stage reasoning that was one below their present stage. Turiel assumed that since a stage displaces the preceding ones by reorganizing them into a more complex structure, it would be likely that the individual exposed to reasoning at one stage below his present stage would reject the lower mode of reasoning. The design of the experiment conducted to test these hypotheses involved a population of forty-four seventh-grade boys, ages twelve and thirteen, chosen randomly from school files. They were divided into four groups. One was exposed to stage reasoning one above (+1) their current dominant stage, a second to reasoning two above (+2) their dominant stage, and a third to reasoning one stage below (−1) their dominant stage. A fourth group served as the control. Kohlberg's moral judgment interview was the instrument used to determine dominant stage in a pretest and in a posttest to assess what gains, if any, had been made.

The method entailed a role-playing procedure which required the subject to assume the role of the main character in the story. He was asked to approach two friends in search of advice on how to resolve the moral dilemma he was faced with. The experimenter simulated the role of both friends. He presented the subject with two opposing solutions, each at the same level of reasoning and at the relative stage appropriate to the particular subject in the experiment. For example, a stage 2 subject playing the role of Heinz would seek advice on whether to steal the drug to save his wife's life or not. If he had been assigned to the +1 group, then the experimenter would present two arguments, one in favor of stealing the drug at Stage 3 and one against stealing at stage 3. The subjects who were chosen to participate in the experiment were at stages 2, 3, and 4. The experimental design permitted deriving two sets of results: one was direct and the other indirect. The former used the same test material in the posttest as had been used in the experiment itself. The latter used the same material in the posttest as had been used in the pretest, but had not been used in the experiment. Turiel's hypotheses were confirmed. Results pertaining to the direct influence were most compelling. Those subjects exposed to +2 showed no influence. Subjects exposed to +1 demonstrated a significant increase in their use of the stage one above what had been their dominant stage. Subjects exposed to −1 did exhibit some influence from this exposure, but their posttest use of one stage below what had been identified as their dominant stage was not nearly as significant as exposure to +1 had been for those in that group. Analysis of indirect influence revealed trends in the same direction, but the weight of the evidence was not as significant as in the analysis of direct influence. Turiel concludes that the results call for a rejection of the notion that the gains could be accounted for merely by the subjects having memorized the advice offered them at a different stage, as this explanation would not account for the differential aspect of the findings. The indirect influence, although weaker than the direct, does suggest some generalization. The fact that exposure to +2 had no effect, whereas exposure to +1 had a significant effect, is taken as evidence in support of Kohlberg's theory of the invariant sequence followed in progressing through moral stages. The ease of assimilating concepts one stage above one's dominant stage and the inability to comprehend reasoning two stages above is exactly what one would predict. The insignificant, but apparent, use of some −1 reasoning by the group exposed to one stage below the dominant stage indicates that lower stages are comprehended, but not especially influential.

Turiel goes on to suggest that cognitive conflict may be the dynamic which produces transition to a significant use of reasoning at one stage above the dominant stage. The structural shift occurs as a result of the conflict inducing disequilibrium, which sets in motion an equilibrating process that eventuates in a new and more adequate equilibrium. The subjects in the experiment, he comments, were not supplied univocal answers to resolve the moral dilemmas. Instead they were offered two contradictory alternatives, both at the same level of moral reasoning, however. The task of resolution remained with the subjects. Turiel suggests that when confronted with the contradictory options, the subjects may have entered a state of cognitive conflict upon contemplating them. The ensuing disequilibrium then resulted in structural development that integrated preceding stages and achieved a higher level of equilibrium. Because +2 arguments could not be comprehended, they did not stimulate conflict. Arguments at −1 did not precipitate conflict because their comparative simplicity was recognized as less adequate than the stage the subject was at currently. It was for those subjects presented with arguments one stage above their dominant stage that the procedure held the most meaning, hence producing conflict as they grappled with the concepts involved. This observation highlights, once again, the significant phenomenological aspect of Kohlberg's work.

Turiel raises the question, in "Developmental Processes in the Child's Moral Thinking," of how it is that a child can grasp the contradiction inherent in opposing arguments that are even only one stage above his own. If, by definition, he is not yet at the next stage, then why is reasoning at that stage not also incomprehensible, just as is the case for stages two or more above the present stage. Cognitive-developmental psychology is rescued from this problem by the reality of stage mixture. Turiel rejects the notion of discrete homogeneous stages sharply demarcated from adjacent stages with development consisting of a sudden leap out of one stage and into the next. Functioning exclusively at one stage would preclude the possibility of apprehending the contradictions inherent in incompatible arguments one stage above. It follows that where there is a relatively low mixture of the dominant stage and some amount of the next stage, development will be slow. The presence of a higher mixture facilitates development, as those elements that are already present from the next stage will facilitate the child's capacity to perceive the contradiction in opposing solutions one stage above his dominant stage. The recognition of the conflict then energizes the equilibrating process toward structural reorganization. Bearing in mind the crucial role of stage mixture, it is worth noting Turiel's incisive comment that "Change occurs when perceived conceptual contradictions energize attempts to restructure by exploring the organizational properties of the higher mode of thought."[8] Following this we find the key to perceiving the contradiction in Turiel's statement:

A child who functioned at only one stage would experience relatively little conflict, as it would be difficult for him to perceive contradictions in the external environment. The child whose functioning is mainly on one

stage, but who uses other stages as well, will more readily perceive contradictions and thus experience conflict more frequently. . . . Stage
mixture serves to facilitate the perception of contradictions, making the
individual more susceptible to disequilibrium and consequently more
likely to progress developmentally.[9]

A deepening appreciation of moral stages and their transitions may
be acquired through familiarity with "Level of Moral Development As
a Determinant of Preference," by Rest, Turiel, and Kohlberg and
Rest's subsequent contribution, "The Hierarchical Nature of Moral
Judgment," which builds upon the former. The first of these two
studies was an attempt to duplicate, through a different design, the
findings of Turiel cited above and to further seek explanatory factors.

The essential difference in the design and the experiment conducted by Rest, Turiel, and Kohlberg was that after being presented
with a moral dilemma, the subjects were provided with six statements giving advice for resolution. The advice was one stage below,
one above, and two above the subjects' own dominant stage. At each
of the three stages there were two opposing pieces of advice. The
subjects were initially scored at a given stage ranging one through
four. Subjects at stage 1 were given advice at their own stage in lieu
of advice one stage below, which would not have been possible. The
subjects ranged in age from ten to fourteen, with an average IQ score
of 119, the lowest being 95 and the highest 150. Rather than being
exposed to opposing arguments at only one stage, these subjects
were exposed to the full gamut of advice covering three stages. The
advice was contained in a booklet and was hypothetically being offered by a variety of friends. The subjects were then asked a series of
questions, such as who gave the best advice and who gave the worst.
Other inquiries sought to determine which of the friends was
thought to be the "smartest" and which the "most good" on the basis
of the advice. Each response was probed to elicit the reasons behind
it, which generally brought forth a restatement of the advice that
could be scored by degree of comprehension. The subjects were also
asked to formulate a version of their own advice.

The findings reflected a consistently significant trend toward selecting statements at higher stages as containing preferred modes of
thought and a correspondingly significant tendency to prefer least the
advice at the lower stage. Comprehension of the stages decreased,
however, in going from lower to higher. Subjects were asked, in

effect, to recapitulate the stage of their preference. Those who selected one stage below their own comprehended it most frequently.
Subjects voicing a preference for one stage above exhibited a moderate frequency of comprehension by comparison. Lastly, those who
preferred advice at two stages above their own were the least
frequently correct in their comprehension of the advice. There was a
marked tendency, when incorrectly recapitulating the advice, to assimilate it at the subjects' own stage or one stage below. In instances
where the advice was disliked, the tendency was to distort it by assimilation specifically to one stage below the subjects' own stage.
Further analysis compared the subjects' own construction of advice
to their pretest scores, after exposure to the friends' advice. The result confirmed Turiel's finding that there is a significant increase in
correct usage of responses at one stage above the subjects' dominant
stage, whereas two stages above had no influence and one stage
below only slight influence. The explanation offered suggests that $+1$
over $-1$ is based on preference, since $-1$ is well comprehended, but
not preferred. Regarding $+1$ over $+2$, it is speculated that comprehension is the critical factor, since $+2$ is not well comprehended, but
both $+1$ and $+2$ are preferred. Rest et al. emphasize that lower-level
stage reasoning is rejected on structural grounds in that the rejecting
subjects comprehend its qualitative character, but still do not prefer
it. Contrary to this, whenever higher-level advice is rejected, the
grounds are not structural. In other words, there was never evidence
that a subject genuinely comprehended higher-stage advice and then
rejected it. When higher advice was rejected, an examination always
revealed an other than structural basis. For example, the subjects
rejecting $+2$ advice very frequently had distorted it to the point that
they had understood it as being $-1$, which interpretation served as
the basis for the rejection. It was also found that liking $+2$ was often
based upon misinterpreting it at the subjects' own stage level or one
above, especially when the content agreed with what the child's own
belief dictated. In such a case, for example, a stage 2 child who
believed the drug should not be stolen (content), might have a tendency to prefer stage 4 advice not to steal the drug. However, it is
revealed upon examination that this child does not comprehend the
stage 4 reasoning, but instead interprets (distorts) it as being at stage
2 or 3 reasoning. There are aspects of the rhetoric of stage 4 that
promote preference for it, but the actual limitations of the stage 2

child's development simply does not permit true structural comprehension.

Rest, in elaborating further upon findings on the hierarchical nature of stage development, maintains that a subject providing evidence of comprehending a stage generally manifests a comprehension of previous stages. Significantly, about half of all subjects studied exhibit comprehension of a stage that is one stage above their own predominant stage as revealed in a pretest. The best predictor of understanding a stage beyond one's predominant stage is the amount of spontaneous usage of a stage beyond the predominant one that the subject is observed expressing. In other words, when scoring a subject for moral stage, it was recognized that in addition to the spontaneous products of the predominant stage to which they were assigned, approximately half of the subjects displayed 20 percent spontaneous usage of higher stages. Of that group, as many as 84 percent understood those stages above their predominant one, which they had used spontaneously. There was a marked difference of only 30 percent, who did not show any spontaneous stage use above the predominant one, providing evidence of comprehending any stages higher than the predominant stage. Reflecting upon the distinction between spontaneous usage of a stage and comprehension of a stage based on advice presented to a subject, Rest points out that the former involves a more mature skill. In spontaneous usage the subject does not merely respond to a formulation that already embodies moral reasoning, but instead he must construct and organize the reasoning on his own. Therefore, subjects showing substantial usage of a higher stage than their predominant one may well be expected to comprehend all stages that they are capable of utilizing spontaneously. Rest's empirical observations lend credence to Turiel's advocacy of stage mixture as critical to undergoing transition in the stage hierarchy. The spontaneous usage of a stage other than the assigned one is generally that of one higher than that which predominates. Hence, when a subject comprehends a stage higher than his predominant one, it will usually be the stage one above. Furthermore, it is those subjects who demonstrate comprehension of one stage above their predominant one who are the most likely to show a decisive shift in the posttest toward increased thinking at one stage higher. Thus, spontaneous usage is predictive of comprehension, which is predictive of assimilation. Rest uses the term assimilation in this context to refer to accurate increase in thinking at the next higher stage above the predominant one upon being exposed to the experimental condition. Lastly, the highest stage comprehended is most likely to be the one preferred from among all those stages that are comprehended. Genuine understanding of the structural components of a stage is likely to compel the subject to embrace it as preferable. There was no tendency to prefer one's own predominant stage. However, Rest maintains that his findings indicate that irrespective of comprehension and spontaneous production of a stage, subjects tended to prefer the higher stages. Stage 6 is preferred the most, stage 5 next and so on in that order. While it is clear that subjects would prefer the highest stage comprehended over all lower stages which are also comprehended, it is not clear why subjects would prefer higher stages not comprehended and do so with a diminishing degree of preference in order, starting with stage 6 as most preferred. Rest speculates upon this phenomenon, offering several possible explanations, but seems to favor a Plantonic doctrine of intuitive recognition of the truly just, despite an absence of ability to either spontaneously articulate or comprehend it. As Kohlberg has stated elsewhere in reflecting Plato's ideas:

> The kind of knowledge of the good which is virtue is philosophical knowledge or intuition of the ideal form of the good, not correct opinion or acceptance of conventional beliefs.
>
> . . . .
>
> The reason the good can be taught is because we know it all along dimly or at a low level and its teaching is more a calling out than an instruction.
>
> The reason we think the good cannot be taught is because the same good is known differently at different levels and direct instruction cannot take place across levels.
>
> Then the teaching of virtue is the asking of questions and the pointing of the way, not the giving of answers. Moral education is the leading of men upward, not the putting into the mind of knowledge that was not there before.[10]

The preceding statements provide a smooth transition into a discussion of Kohlberg's considerable efforts at utilizing the findings on hierarchical stage development in the field of moral education. Kohlberg has frequently acknowledged a great debt to John Dewey, the American philosopher of pragmatism or instrumentalism, for influencing his thoughts on moral development and education. Before proceeding further, a brief sketch of Dewey's influence would be appropriate. Dewey (1859–1952) was profoundly interested in the connection between science and values. He rejected the bifurcation proposed by those who held that values had no place in the matrix of scientific beliefs. He has stated, in thoughts that may reveal some of his strong appeal for Kohlberg, the following:

> The problem of restoring integration and cooperation between man's beliefs about the world in which he lives and his beliefs about values and purposes that should direct his conduct is the deepest problem of modern life. It is the problem of any philosophy that is not isolated from life.[11]

In another incisive comment, alluding to the concern between thought and action, Dewey formulates the following:

> A moral situation is one in which judgment and choice are required antecedently to overt action. The practical meaning of the situation—that is to say the action needed to satisfy it—is not self-evident. It has to be searched for. There are conflicting desires and alternative apparent goods. What is needed is to find the right course of action, the right good. Hence inquiry is exacted. . . . This inquiry is intelligence. . . .[12]

Dewey placed great faith in the educational system as the avenue through which moral education should take place. He advocated a democratic milieu with emphasis upon persuasion, reason, interaction, and in brief, the process as the essential ingredient for growth, a desirable end in itself. For Dewey, moral principles were not ethereal and inert abstractions that existed in a realm remote from everyday life. Although real, they had meaning for him only insofar as they infused the lives of individuals, embracing them in a community context. Applied to the school curriculum, geography, for example, was not to be taught simply as a body of facts about the earth, but in a way that organized and related those facts to human, value-laden concerns. Dewey's view, echoed in Kohlberg's position today, is that if the school is to prepare one for properly living in a democratic, social, and moral manner upon graduation, then it must recreate the conditions necessary for such a life. It cannot reasonably expect to subject children and adolescents to twelve years of authoritarian rule in a morally sterile context and then set them free to lead their lives as committed adults participating in the democratic process. Dewey sees education as development and Kohlberg seizes upon this to assert with some congency that, therefore, once one knows what development actually is, he then has a loadstone to help construct a definition of what it ought to be. For Dewey and Kohlberg, experience is intrinsic to development. It is the responsibility of the schools to provide those experiences which will stimulate development upward through the stages in the hierarchy toward more adequate functioning. Kohlberg is adamant in rejecting any suggestion that the schools should teach children conformity to conventional rules and authoritative pronouncements, as their primary goal of moral education. He is equally assertive in challenging the prevalent philosophical posture of engendering an acceptance of ethical relativity among children. He has taken pains to expose the "hidden curriculum" in schools, making it clear that if not explicit, then values will be implicit in the child's school experience. Lastly, as has been alluded to previously, the "bag of virtues" approach, still popular today and promulgated by no less an ancient sage than Aristotle, is roundly rejected by Kohlberg. The proper role of the school is to create that milieu which will stimulate cognitive and moral development as far along the universal stage hierarchy as possible for each student. It is not simply because later stages come after earlier stages that Kohlberg pronounces them better. They constitute a proper aim for moral education because:

> What is most properly called development is a movement toward greater adaptation, differentiation, and integration. Each stage is a more differentiated, comprehensive, and integrated or equilibrated structure than its predecessor, and the fundamental cause of movement from one stage to the next is that a later stage is better, more adequate in some universal sense, than an earlier stage. . . . My psychological theory for explaining why children move from one moral stage to the next is built upon a philosophic or ethical theory in which each higher stage is morally and logically more adequate than the one below.[13]

The above statement by Kohlberg is the most direct and succinct formulation that one will find in his voluminous writings to support, on theoretical grounds, his position on why higher stages are better and why, therefore, their attainment should be the aim of education. He is unrelenting in his conviction that moral education as he conceives it is not, even remotely, to be equated with indoctrination. The emphasis is upon the form of moral reasoning and not upon content or telling the child what to believe. The mode of education he is advocating does not single out any particular religious or sociopolitical ideology.

Kohlberg has been engaged in direct intervention within school systems on an experimental basis. On a micro-level he has been instrumental in activities involving classroom discussions designed to facilitate development of the discussants. The method is to present hypothetical moral dilemmas with the leader introducing arguments one stage above the stage of the students whose stage is lowest in the class. The premise is that for those students the discussion induces dissatisfaction with their own resolutions. An ensuing cognitive dissonance promotes the disequilibrium that engenders a reorganization and restructuring at the next highest stage. As the discussions proceed and lower-stage students move upward, the leader increases the stage level of his arguments. On a macro-level, Kohlberg has designed alternative schools which have heightened the engagement of students in participatory democracy, increasing role-taking opportunities in the process. Emphasis is upon discussions and decision making around issues vital to the students, such as drugs, from the standpoint of morality and fairness. Kohlberg has been critical of the schools' moral climate, which he contests too often is based upon stage 1, obedience and punishment orientation, and stage 4, law and order orientation.

## LOGIC AND MORAL JUDGMENT

Kohlberg has made it clear that he does not view moral judgment as merely the application of logic to the moral domain. The justice structure that is constructed and reconstructed throughout development has an essential nature of its own that makes it separable from the purely logical. However, moral judgment at any given stage has a structural quality parallel to and dependent upon the structure of cognition at corresponding periods of development. Cognitive development, therefore, places constraints upon the range of one's moral judgment and is considered to be a necessary, but not sufficient condition for it. There appear to be two major critical points in the influence brought to bear by cognitive transformations upon moral development. The first is the presence of concrete operations which promotes moral judgment at stage 2. Prior to the emergence of the concrete operational period, the child's moral judgment is not likely to exceed the punishment and obedience orientation of stage 1. The second critical development is the emergence of formal operations necessary for the social contract orientation of stage 5. Kuhn, Langer, Kohlberg, Haan, in "The Development of Formal Operations in Logical and Moral Judgment," maintain that subjects who display some principled moral reasoning, but are at an incipient phase of emerging formal operations, are still found to be predominantly at stage 4. The early emergence of formal operational thought, they have found, is necessary for the consolidation of a pure stage 4 development. However, some conventional moral reasoning exists without the presence of formal operations. Concrete operational subjects never demonstrate moral judgment responses that exceeded stage 4. Most subjects at the concrete operational period or lower exhibit moral reasoning that is predominantly stage 3 or below. Completely or predominantly moral thinking at the principled level does not become consolidated until the later stages of formal operations have appeared. Kuhn et al. believe that paramount to their findings was the observed décalage between purely cognitive and moral spheres. In one sample only 21 percent evidence some principled thought, out of 85 percent who showed some formal operational thought. In a second group there was evidence of 9 percent demonstrating some principled thought, out of a total of 80 percent who demonstrated some formal operations. In general, substantial moral growth occurred during the earlier stages of development. Once subjects reach the conventional level, advance in moral judgment is found with diminished frequency. Thus, it seems that logical structural development progresses further than does moral maturity in most cases. Keasey in a review of studies on the subject under discussion, "Implications of Cognitive Development for Moral Reasoning," reached the conclusion that the evidence supports adopting the position on cognitive development as a necessary condition for moral development and that the former facilitates the emergence of the latter, although is not sufficient to fully account for it.

Kuhn et al. attempted to fill in the gap between formal operations and principled moral judgment. To accomplish this they focused upon those of their adult and adolescent subjects who were predominantly formal operational, with the aim of comparing those who had achieved principled moral judgment to those who had not. Their strategy was to identify the presence or absence of two additional variables. These were social order concepts and moral comprehension. In a commentary upon the former, they state:

> We are interested . . . in when an S makes the transition from a conception of the social order in which societal regulation is maintained for its own sake, to a conception of the social order in which societal regulation has as its purpose the protection of individual welfare and rights. Our purpose . . . was to investigate this transition in conception of the social order itself, as distinguished from the transition in moral judgment we think it generates.[14]

The critical transition being referred to, of course, is from stage 4 to stage 5. Social order concepts are viewed as being more immediately linked to logical operations. Moral comprehension is seen as more directly connected to moral judgment. Since moral judgments presented to subjects can be comprehended before the subjects can spontaneously express them, it is assumed that competence at comprehension would be a necessary element in a continuum of elements, which would precede spontaneous moral judgment. The proposed order of elements in the continuum is as follows: logical operations, social order concepts, moral comprehension, spontaneous moral judgment. The expectation in this formulation is that whenever the presence of a latter element is identified, the preceding elements would also always be present. However, identification of a given element would not automatically assure that those which follow are present. Kuhn et al. conclude from this portion of their study that the evidence is suggestive of such a continuum, but urge that further research is necessary for elaboration and confirmation. At the risk of confusion, but in the hope of avoiding oversimplification, it must not be thought that the influence of one mental structure upon another is always unidirectional. Kuhn et al. point out that each mental structure functions within two domains. It interacts with the structure of the environment, but it also interacts internally with other mental structures. As has been commented upon in previous sections, when interaction produces feedback that is discrepant with the initiating mental structure, then a disequilibrium is induced and is resolved by structures reorganizing at a higher level. Reflecting the reverberating complexities that can occur in the course of development, Kuhn et al. explicate the following:

> An interaction between a given mental structure and the environment . . . may stimulate a reorganization in the internal relationship or coor-

dination of this structure and other related structures. This reorganization in turn may generate internal disequilibrium which leads to further interactions with the environment, involving both the original and related structures.

. . . Mental operations, in the purely logical domain should influence operations in more peripheral domains more so than the reverse. This influence, however, is not strictly unilateral; cognitive operations are only adequately described as a network of interactive and coregulative structures.[15]

Thus, Kuhn et al. suggest that despite the ordered sequence they tentatively put forth to explain the development of moral judgment, there probably occurs a bidirectional interplay among the various domains of the mental structures.

The study by Kuhn et al. is a most ambitious one. They utilized two samples, one comprised of 265 adults and adolescents, the other of 75 youngsters from ten to twelve years of age. The preadolescents were involved in a short-term longitudinal study spanning a nine-month period. Cognitive development was assessed through testing with three Piagetian tasks. These were the pendulum problem, a correlation situation involving a set of cards, and the chemicals problem requiring combinatorial analysis. Moral judgment was determined by use of the Kohlberg interview. It is worth noting that among adults in the sample, 15 percent failed to demonstrate any formal operational thought. There were 30 percent who had crystalized their cognitive competence at the formal operational period. The majority, 55 percent, were in a transitional state between concrete and formal operations.

Emphasis in the Kuhn et al. study was upon the qualitative correspondence between logical and moral domains and not upon mere correlational discoveries. They explored the increasing differentiation between what "is" and what "ought" to be, the full blooming of which becomes possible upon the consolidation of the formal operational thought structures. The stage 4 moral reasoner, in emphasizing the maintenance of laws, is fusing the factual character of laws with what ought to be. He has not yet achieved the formal operational thinkers recognition that what is, is merely one subset of a range covering the gamut of what is possible. He is more advanced, however, than those at earlier stages, for at least in the face of law violations, the law does stand as that which ought to have been followed rather than the fact of the transgressors' behavior. Once formal

operations become firmly established there is an essential reversal in
that the thinker grasps that reality is one possibility among many.
The law need not be maintained as it is and new laws may be formed
guided by one's vision of what ought to be. The capacity for second
order operations of the final period of cognitive development facilitates the individual's progression in his judgment making capacity.
As Kuhn et al. state:

> Initially the S only makes judgments of fact, what is. He then becomes
> capable of making judgments about the fact: i.e., norms or rules apply-
> ing to fact. Only at the most advanced level does he become capable of
> second-order operations: operations on operations, or judgments about
> judgments.[16]

In other words, there is a structural isomorphism between the secon-
dary-order logical operations which constitute a central feature of the
formal operational period and the principled-level individual's new
found competence at making second-order moral judgments. A final
differentiation must occur at the principled level. Even though the
stage 5 moral reasoner has shifted from a law-maintaining to a law-
creating creature, Kuhn et al. stress that the moral oughts are still
not fully universalized as they are locked into the procedural mechanism which is the hallmark of the social contract orientation. When
this final differentiation is made, then the individual is completely autonomous in choosing a priori universal oughts based upon natural
rights. These are rights which, Kuhn et al. assert,

> . . . can be phrased in terms of liberty, equality, and reciprocity or sim-
> ply in terms of the concept of the equal worth of all human beings as
> ends in themselves, rather than means.[17]

The Kohlbergian autonomous individual is rare, but he does exist. To
achieve that autonomy, however, he must first undergo a cognitive
transformation. Grounded in the power of formal operational thought,
he soars to the highest moral principles.

# Chapter Six

# Methodological and Theoretical Critique

The work of Kohlberg has been criticized both by enemies who seek to deliver mortal blows and by friends who aim to effect improvement. In the case of the former, attack is usually leveled against the heart of the theory. Propositions bearing upon the invariance of stage sequence, the hierarchical nature of the stages, and their universality are challenged. In more friendly quarters, methodological shortcomings are cited and accompanied by recommendations. The limitations of the theory, with its deemphasis upon affect and habit, traditional components of moral psychology, are highlighted as the congenial critic generally urges movement in the direction of integrating cognitive, affective, and behavioral elements. Inquiries are made about the extent to which Kohlberg has abandoned the scientific foundation of his work in favor of philosophical speculations which have led him to advocate an impossible ideal that may be more an expression of his own bias than the objective truth he claims it to be. Although published articles by Kohlberg and his collaborators are numerous, a published volume by him devoted exclusively to his theory and research findings has not yet been made available. In view of the impact and scope of Kohlberg's achievement, the lack of such a publication has represented a serious deficiency. However, over the last several years he has been listing two forthcoming books in his bibliographies. In personal communication with the Harvard Center for Moral Education, I was informed in the summer of 1978 that a three-volume work edited by Kohlberg is expected to be published within approximately one year.

An extensive theoretical exposition encompassing the sophistication and complexity of Kohlberg's work, as well as abundant citation of its empirical moorings, appears in the preceding chapters. Therefore, I shall not attempt here to marshal a defense of his unquestionably significant and far-reaching efforts. Instead, an endeavor will be made to maintain fidelity to the critical sources which have attempted to cast a spotlight upon possible weaknesses in Kohlberg's system.

Peters, in "Moral Development," has taken issue with Kohlberg for staunchly maintaining a monolithic position to the exclusion of other schools of thought which have traditionally contributed to moral psychology. The form of justice, so narrowly constricting Kohlberg's conception of morality, implies other values which are never considered within the system. To determine what is just on a substantive issue necessitates introducing other criteria which in themselves could assume greater priority in an alternate moral system. Peters speaks specifically of attempting to determine what might be a just wage, which entails considering factors such as need, contribution to community, and risk involved. These veer in the direction of content over form, Peters suggests, and to that extent, Kohlberg's system must move toward being prescriptive. Remaining with an emphasis upon form over content and avoiding this horn of the dilemma places Kohlberg on the other horn of being too formal to guide moral educators or ethical agents in everyday life. In extending further his comments on the distinction between form and content, Peters agrees that Kohlberg is correct in maintaining that a form of cognitive stimulation or Socratic dialectic is necessary for generating principles in the learner. However, he goes on to emphasize that there is a place for teaching in the area of content, as well, and this would rely upon the direct showing and telling of the teacher, which Kohlberg seems to belittle.

Peters insists that certain essential trait-like characteristics must be accounted for in a fashion that is different from how the development of justice principles is accounted for. Concern for others is vital to moral character and yet this precedes conceptions of justice in very young children, even though this concern may later be ordered along the lines of justice. He distinguishes a category of traits which, unlike honesty, is content-free and necessary if the will to abide by one's principles is to be present. This category encompasses such traits as courage, integrity, determination, consistency, and persistence. Devoid of these elements of will, the most principled moral thinker would be sterile as an ethical agent in his encounter with the real world. Peters outlines a hierarchy of traits ranging from those that are rooted to specific acts, such as punctuality, to the higher-order traits identified above, which are not linked to specific acts. Implied in all of them, however, are principles. Punctuality may be a mechanically learned trait, but implied by it as an objectively desirable act, it could be argued, is a consideration for the rights and feelings of other people. Peters is of the opinion that in maintaining a sharp dichotomy between principles and traits, Kohlberg has exaggerated the difference and created an artificial distinction. In any event, Kohlberg's criticism of character traits, in Peters view, is limited to those that are most concretely involved with specific acts, such as honesty, and overlooks others along the scale, such as compassion.

The central thrust of Peters' criticism concentrates upon Kohlberg's relegation of habit formation to a role of minor importance in moral development. The virtuous traits, which Kohlberg slights, are cultivated by habit formation. Aristotle long ago underscored the need to practice virtue in order to develop and bring it to maturity. Virtuous actions, to be sure, will not be appreciated for what they are by the very young. External rewards and punishments certainly will play a role in training the very young. However, this is necessary if the correct behaviors are to be carried out. In time, the inner understanding and motives to do the right thing for the right reason will hopefully appear. In Peters's view habit formation constitutes the early pole of a continuum leading to a mature virtuous morality that is informed by reason. Acquired initially through external incentives provided by the caretakers, the child will eventually appreciate the reason in ethical terms for maintaining that which is virtuous. In this formulation, reason supports what has had its origin in habit, but does not substitute for it. Intelligence can be applied to habit in the sense of thinking about one's actions that derive from habits. In brief, one can acquire the habit of honest behavior to avoid punishment and later, even in the absence of possible punitive consequences, maintain honest behavior with a full appreciation of its desirability in interpersonal terms, as one reflects upon it. Reason then reenforces the early acquired honest behaviors and, hence, habit and reason work in tandem. Children when very young cannot comprehend a principle so abstract as justice, nor even recognize that certain rules derive their raison d'être from principles. This is where habituation enters. Through exposure and repetition one may acquire certain action patterns. Habituation may occur as the result of associative learning or through intentional design. In habituating the very young to certain virtuous acts, such as honesty, there must be some attempt to explain to the child what the relevant acts and contexts are. Habituation in the moral sphere must be accompanied by understanding at the appropriate level for moral education to occur. The point Peters seeks to make is that habit in children need not be acquired by a process of drill, but through one in which the connections between rules, as well as their consequences, are consistently brought to their attention. In a brief summary of this aspect of his position, Peters states, "My argument is that learning habits in an intelligent way can be regarded as providing an appropriate basis, in the moral case, for the later stage when rules are followed or rejected because of the justification that they are seen to have or lack."[1]

Peters further develops his argument by suggesting that Kohlberg has been so preoccupied with the abstract virtue of justice that he has ignored an important but somewhat less abstract virtue. Much more meaningful for young children at their stage of development than the concept of justice is concern for others. Peters suggests, "The plight of others is much easier to grasp, and concern for it develops much earlier in children. If such concern is encouraged early in children, it can come to function later as one of the fundamental principles of morality, when the child reaches the stage of being able to grasp the connection between many rules and their effect on other people."[2] Principled morality is barren without the proper sensitivity to people's suffering which might move one to action. Young children can be trained to decenter from their own concerns and to also take into account the needs of others. An habituation to doing so may generate a compassionate disposition, which in turn may produce appropriately relevant moral actions in response to human suffering.

Virtues of self-control, which Kohlberg fails to consider, are for Peters those of the highest order. They have already been identified as courage, determination, persistence, integrity, and consistency. If one is to possess the moral courage to act upon principle, then there must be some training in acquiring such courage to face rebuke and ostracism from the social milieu, in the course of growing up. It is precisely this type of character training that will sustain the autonomous principled thinker when confronted with the inevitability of social resistance and confrontation. There can be very little autonomy for the principled thinker who does not possess moral courage. In fact, to reason at a principled level without the courage to sustain one's convictions may induce great stress and guilt.

In conclusion, there is something of a paradox contained in the observations made by Peters. He has insisted that the basic concepts of habit and trait be accorded their proper place in moral psychology, despite Kohlberg's almost contemptuous dismissal of what he calls a "bag of virtues." In doing so, Peters has restored to moral psychology some of the grand traditional notions, such as moral courage and integrity, which Kohlberg's exclusive emphasis on justice has eliminated. There is one final component omitted from Kohlberg's work, which Peters comments upon with almost chilling simplicity. It is one thing to know the difference between right and wrong. It is quite another to care.

Alston, in "Comments on Kohlberg's 'From Is to Ought,' " has also commented upon Kohlberg's neglect of the concept of habit, as well as his deemphasis of affect in the moral system. That both habit and affect have been consigned to roles of secondary importance is viewed as an artifact of the moral dilemmas, used in the interview, which are designed in a fashion that assures channeling the subject's responses in a cognitive direction. Alston takes Kohlberg to task for having asserted that conflict between physical desires and conscience poses no real moral crisis, in contrast to the view that moral crisis derives from uncertainty in social situations when one experiences a disintegration of moral expectations. Alston's point is simply that only a biased ideological commitment could lead to this sort of one-sided positon, when clearly a moral crisis could be precipitated in the individual faced with either condition.

Alston construes being at a moral stage as evidencing an "habitual style of moral" reasoning. He concedes that the child who moralizes at a certain stage must have acquired the concept commensurate with that stage. However, he challenges that this provides adequate grounds for inferring anything about concept development. The frequent use of concepts at a certain level is not proof that concepts at higher levels not being used are necessarily absent. A concept may be present in a behavioral repetoire, but dormant. Citing Kohlberg's own acknowledgment that about 50 percent of one's concepts in moral reasoning derives from stages adjacent to the predominant stage, Alston chips away at how meaningful it really is to say that someone is at a certain stage. An individual may very well have the higher concepts, but find it more natural to reason at lower stages. Hence the reason for that individual's being assigned to the lower stage is different from what is ordinarily assumed by Kohlbergians. Alston is not adverse to accepting the invariant stage theory of moral development, but is urging that a more rigorous test to determine what concepts one truly does and does not possess be designed, with less emphasis upon concept tendencies expressed in overt verbal reasoning. Current adversaries of the cognitive-developmental field consistently make the argument that performance at a certain level in a cognitive task does not rule out the possibility of competence existing, but unutilized, at a higher level. Conversely, the lack of performance at a given level is not sufficient proof that the competence is not possessed, only that it has not been displayed in a particular task.

Kohlberg has claimed that there is a logical necessity to the order of stage sequences, as increasing differentiation and integration occurs with each stage transition and attainment. Alston is clear, however, that even though this may be so, it offers no support to the position that later stages are morally superior to earlier stages. A concept may be logically contingent for its emergence upon a preceding concept, but it would be a gratuitous leap to assume its moral superiority on that account. Believing it to be a serious challenge to Kohlberg's theory, Alston argues that many philosophers enjoy as much sophistication on a conceptual plane as the stage 6 thinker, yet adopt philosophical and theological positions that correspond to stages 4 and 5. The prescriptive "ought" of Kohlberg's stage is not self-evident, but reflects the built-in bias that has led him in the direction he has pursued. It is incumbent upon him, as with any philosopher, to marshal proof of the superiority of his conception of what is truly moral in the highest sense. Somewhat trenchantly, Alston drives his point home.

> It is notorious that moral philosophers agree no more about what is distinctive of the moral than about anything else; and a large number of distinct accounts of what makes a judgment, a reason, an attitude, a

rule, or a principle, *moral* have been put forth. Kohlberg chooses one of these . . . but fails to do anything by way of showing that this is more than a choice of what seems most congenial or interesting to him. . . . If these pronouncements are to carry any weight, he will have to show that this sense of "moral" which is functioning as his standard has itself some recommendation other than congeniality to his predilections.

What Kohlberg really wants most to recommend to our acceptance is the principle of justice (in his interpretation) as a supreme moral principle. But stages of prescriptivity will not advance that cause. A judgment based on a principle of racial destiny, or no principle at all, can be just as prescriptive as a judgment based on an application of Kohlberg's principle of justice.[3]

Despite Alston's almost unrelenting commentary on Kohlberg's claims, he does temper his remarks by conveying a belief that Kohlberg has contributed to enhancing the field of moral psychology generally and has personally provided Alston with new ways of viewing the field.

In a systematic and searching critique "Moral Development Research," Simpson has pursued further some of Alston's earlier references to Kohlberg's subjectivity. She views Kohlberg as both culture-bound and personally influenced by certain thinkers of his time. A well-aimed arrow strikes directly at the heart of his claim to having established the universality of principled moral reasoning on a scientific basis. Simpson contends that throughout the prodigious body of work produced by Kohlberg, he is fuzzy on the distinction between valid empirical evidence and his own purely normative pronouncements on what he thinks ought to prevail in the moral realm. In other words, it begins to look as if Kohlberg is the least scientific when he is the most prescriptive. Despite his insistence on the commonality of peoples across all cultures, Simpson is equally insistent that Kohlberg has received his intellectual nourishment from the following heroes of Western philosophy: Kant, Mill, Hare, Ross, Dewey, and Rawls. However, the intellectual heritage of Eastern philosophies is essentially different from these sources and Kohlberg fails to take it into consideration in his description of normative ethics. Assuming that it is a logical possibility, a universal normative morality would have to be derived from a synthesis of both Eastern and Western philosophies.

In a pointed commentary on the individualistic and far from universal outlook of Kohlberg, Simpson states the following:

Like each of us, Kohlberg himself, his interest in cognitive development and moral reasoning, his choice of a Kantian or Deweyian infrastructure for this theory and his predilection for abstractions of such principles as justice, equality, and reciprocity are all, in a sense, accidents of time and place and the interaction of his personality with a specifiable social environment and the norms of the sub-groups within that environment. His rebuttal of Brandt and others who emphasize cultural differences . . . is more a statement of faith than an evidence-based conclusion.[4]

Simpson has argued that despite having research data on at least twelve different cultures, at the time of her remarks, Kohlberg's treatment of his material lacks a sufficient sense of differentiation in comparing these cultures. Furthermore, some of his most dogmatic statements about the universality of postconventional morality are laden with sermonizing phrases rather than scientific ones. In suggesting that under the proper conditions all people, not only the few who have been discovered, would develop to the highest sociomoral level, Kohlberg employs such phrases as "I prefer to think" and "I believe all should." Simpson notes that in so doing Kohlberg clearly reveals the source of his version of normative ethics as personal. He has gone, in Simpson's opinion, from the scientist to the philosopher to the preacher. The indictment is a serious and harsh one, considering the articulated premises from which Kohlberg claims to be building upon.

In his emphasis upon universality and invariant sequence of stages, Kohlberg has minimized, Simpson contends, the very real and profound impact of sociocultural forces. She illustrates this persuasively by an example citing the shift from four- to five-year-olds who do not appear to verbalize that copying other people's work is bad, to six-year-olds who state that it is wrong to do so. Her point is that it is unwarranted to interpret this shift as a natural progression, when the children are going from a preschool orientation of cooperation into a school milieu of competitiveness that honors individual effort over team work. Introducing the variable of competitiveness confounds the findings and demands further research to achieve more certain conclusions. She suggests, further, that the experiential reality of living in a ghetto will rivet the Stage 2 child to an orientation of instrumental relativism. An orientation of this type has functional survival value which will preempt the influence of any natural developmental process. To assume that there exists an autonomous person who is guided by self-chosen universal principles which entirely transcend his sociocultural anchoring is unwarranted. Simpson reasons that the social base of the conventional thinker is apparent because he shares the dominant value system of the society in which he lives. However, the so-called autonomous person may be no freer than those planted in the conventional soil from which he is said to have grown. Observe Simpson's comments on the subject:

> At the post-conventional level the principles displayed may simply be the learned values of a *different* and *smaller* reference group so well internalized that its members believe themselves to be functioning autonomously. . . . In some groups, internality—in the sense of autonomy in respect to the dominant culture—is learned as a norm, and admission and continued membership are contingent upon that knowledge.[5]

A few passages beyond this, she crisply concludes:

> Kohlberg's stage 6s are not functioning independently of their socialization; they have been very thoroughly socialized into the company of intellectual elites who value and practice analytic, abstract, and logical reasoning.[6]

Simpson is doubtful that there exists a level of moral achievement beyond the conventional mode of thought. At least, she contends that the case for Kohlberg's morally autonomous man remains unproven.

In addition to all of the above, Simpson has also found cause to rebuke Kohlberg for what she judges to be his rather discursive method of reporting his own findings. He has failed to follow adequately the canons of explicit and parsimonious reporting of the research he has conducted. Allusions to cross-cultural research, although frequent, do not include appropriate details on samples and methodology. Especially painful is the omission of comments on how the moral dilemma stories are adapted to the various cultures studied. It is essential that the manner in which responses are scored to take into account cultural variations be conveyed. Simpson laments the fact that information in this area has not been made available.[7] It is her opinion that Kohlberg has drawn generalizations from his work that are premature. Replications and methodical research ranging across a greater diversity of the world's cultures must be awaited.

Kurtines and Grief have also questioned that Kohlberg has established the empirical validity of his basic premises in "The Development of Moral Thought." Their critique is a highly technical one which is essentially an assault upon various aspects of the measuring instrument, the Moral Judgment Scale. They allow that refinement of the means for measurement and greater consistency in its application may ultimately confirm Kohlberg's theory, but hold that this is an achievement not yet attained. A restriction placed upon wide use of the instrument is the complexity of administration and scoring it entails. Since the scoring requires an analysis of the subject's responses and is not immediately evident from the responses themselves, special training is necessary and this is provided by Kohlberg himself. Training is offered at summer workshops mounted at the Harvard Center for Moral Education.

The nine moral dilemmas constituting the Moral Judgment Scale are usually not all employed in a given research project and often published reports do not communicate which of the several have been utilized. In addition, since there occurs a clinical probing of subjects' responses during the interviewing, the questions asked will frequently vary from subject to subject. Kurtines and Grief see this lack of standardization in administering the tests as a serious impediment to sound comparisons of research reports. It also raises questions about the validity of generalizations from even a single project. Clearly this does not pose an unsurmountable problem, for at least there can be standardization with regard to which stories would be administered across studies. Kurtines and Grief believe that the chances for rater bias are high because of the judgmental component necessary for scoring and they further suggest that independent research is inhibited due to the scoring difficulties involved. There are also content-oriented problems cited in the Moral Judgment Scale. For example, the fact that most of the characters in the dilemma are male may yield specific moral judgments that are based on a cultural understanding of a differential in sex roles. The reliability of the instrument has not been satisfactorily demonstrated, in the opinion of Kurtines and Grief. Kohlberg has reported interrater reliability for the Moral Judgment Scale. However, a good many of subsequent research projects rely on his former account of this and do not attempt independent efforts to demonstrate such reliability. It is suggested by Kurtines and Grief that it would further understanding and appreciation of each new study if independent interrater reliability measurements bearing on the current research were to be reported. A significant flaw found in all published studies based upon the Moral Judgment Scale, according to Kurtines and Grief, has been the omission of reports on the temporal stability of subjects' responses. It is crucial to Kohlberg's theory that there be accuracy in assigning a subject to a particular stage. Yet there is no evidence that stability of moral judgments by subjects is maintained over brief periods from time $x$ to time $y$. Further, there have been no attempts reported to establish internal consistency across dilemmas, which might provide some assurance that there is a fundamental similarity in what is being measured (i.e., moral reasoning) by them. Kurtines and Grief assert that if they measure basically different domains, then a combined score of virtually unique areas does not add up to meaningful information. Lastly, despite its utility for the Moral Judgment Scale, omitted from the literature are estimates of the standard error of measurement. The authors have pointed out that this would be a particular asset in the field of moral development since a moral stage may reflect only 45 percent judgments at that stage, with the balance being at adjacent stages, the lower stage generally comprising more responses than the higher one.

Another aspect that comes under fire in the Kohlbergian system is what Kurtines and Grief view as its relatively low predictive validity. They recognize that theoretically two people at the same stage may choose alternate courses of action, and also that six individuals, each at a different stage, may all choose the same course of action. Nevertheless, it is true that Kohlberg maintains that there exists a probable relationship between moral stage and action. A survey of the literature led Kurtines and Grief to conclude that the predictive validity of the theory in this regard is moderate at best, when comparing grossly between high-level mature moral reasoning and relatively low-level reasoning. A clear correspondence, however, between a specific stage and a predictable action has not been established. They found it particularly difficult to discriminate among the last three stages when it comes to predictive ability, as reflected in the extant literature. Lastly, upon surveying the various types of evidence bearing upon the invariant sequence hypothesis and the hypothesis of qualitatively different structural modes or reasoning, Kurtines and Grief conclude that there does not exist unequivocal support for these hypotheses. Kuhn has responded to this allegation with some counterevidence and the following observation:

> . . . : it is probably fair to say that Kurtines and Grief . . . have recognized neither the complexity of the task nor the uniqueness of Kohlberg's theoretical sequence. . . . To obtain the appropriate longitudinal

data is a formidable task, especially in the case of the more advanced portion of the sequence, where progress, Kohlberg claims, is slow and not all individuals complete the progression. But the theoretical model should not be rejected until these data have been obtained.[8]

The dialectical process in search of truth will most likely continue for some time to come. In fact, Broughton has already offered a thorough negation of the negation by Kurtines and Grief in "The Cognitive-Developmental Approach to Morality."

An arresting reformulation of Kohlberg's stage theory has been recently advanced by Gibbs in "Kohlberg's Stages of Moral Judgment." He first cites two criteria, previously identified by Piaget, for qualification as a naturalistic stage theory. One of them is simply that stages should be found commonly among all peoples. The other is that behavior emanating from the stages derive from processes which the individual is not conscious of. It is Gibbs's contention that these criteria, applied to the first four stages of Kohlberg's theory, qualify them as candidates for constituting a naturalistic stage theory. He sets apart the last two stages, however, as distinctly different. They are referred to as existential themes, lacking in universality, and characterized by "meta-ethical reflection." Upon reviewing the literature which mostly focuses upon the first four stages, Gibbs firmly concludes that these stages do, indeed, meet all of the Piagetian stage criteria. Gibbs further suggests that Kohlberg's theory embraces holism, constructivism, and interactionism. Each of these is a major characterization of Piaget's cognitive-structural developmental theory. Naturalism, also a Piagetian characteristic, is not entirely applied by Kohlberg to his theory. Naturalism stresses continuity between species and the biological roots of human functioning. According to Gibbs, this also implies a cognitive unconscious which, indeed, Piaget has cited in "Affective Unconscious and Cognitive Unconscious."

The principled level of morality is one in which the member takes a stand or perspective outside of society and reflectively questions conventional morality. The rarity of principled thinking raises doubts about whether it is comprised of what may be said to meet the Piagetian stage criteria, as do the first four stages of Kohlberg's theory. In addition to being found with reasonable frequency, naturalistic stages should have a tendency to move upward through sequences and they should respond to enrichment in the social milieu with increased progress. Doubt is also raised because the reflective nature of principled morality imparts a dimension of self-consciousness not present in naturalistic stages, as interpreted by Gibbs. He states, "Post-conventionality is the existential experience of disembedding oneself from an implicit worldview and adopting a detached and questioning posture."[9] At the principled level there is an attempt to consciously formalize philosophies which are implicit in earlier stages. Gibbs does not construe stages 5 and 6 as integrating and replacing previous stages in the same way that, for example, stage 3 reorganizes and subsumes stage 2. At the same time he fully affirms that, confronted with an unjust situation, principled thinking may govern behavior and in so doing preempt the earlier naturalistic stages. Moral thinkers at the principled level confronted with injustice, ". . . have experienced a dissonance between ethical presuppositions and the demands of their social situations. This conflict may provoke considerable meta-ethical reflection in the effort to formulate a defensible ethic."[10] Gibbs's speculation that a sharp break be recognized between the first four Kohlbergian stages, comprising a naturalistic developmental stage theory, and the last two stages, comprising existential themes, is both abstruse and intriguing. It holds some promise for resolving the issue of accounting for the uncommon appearance of stages 5 and 6 in a theory that purports to validate the universality of stages.

Hall and Davis, like Gibbs, are constructive and congenial critics. As shown in *Moral Education in Theory and Practice,* they find Kohlberg's theory largely impressive, compelling, and therefore, acceptable. In general, however, they find more clarity and persuasiveness in the three basic levels of egocentricity, heteronomy, and autonomy equivalent to the preconventional, conventional, and postconventional levels respectively, than in the descriptions of the six discrete stages. Despite their adoption of his moral developmental theory for their purposes of moral education, they distinguish sharply between his philosophy and psychology, rejecting the former and embracing the latter. Considering the extent to which Kohlberg interweaves, sometimes almost imperceptibly, between philosophy and psychology, this is an important point of difference. Acknowledging the pragmatic value of Kohlberg's theory and believing that it is the best that cognitive-developmental psychology has to offer thus far, Hall and Davis caution against prematurely accepting it with finality. As with many other critics, they are impressed with research validating the invariance of developmental sequences up to stage 4.

Hall and Davis appear to find an inconsistency between Kohlberg's description of a stage as a world view which interprets all experiences through its characteristic mode of thought and the notion of its being inadequate to incorporate some experiences, thereby precipitating the conflict that leads to stage transition. For some reason, which I do not think is made clear, Hall and Davis believe that if it is true that a stage cannot incorporate a particular experience and this precipitates a stage transition, then a social learning model can be invoked to explain the change. The equilibration model is dismissed summarily.

Regarding the issue of generality and specificity, Hall and Davis suggest the interesting notion that one stage may be brought to bear upon specific kinds of issues, whereas another stage, within the same individual, might be brought to bear upon other kinds of issues. The research problem would be to determine what variables influence such a differential functioning of stages. The phenomenon of stage mixture lends some credence to the plausibility of this idea.

Hall and Davis believe that Kohlberg has been less than precise in conveying exactly what he means by stage 6 as the embodiment of a general concept of justice. They note that he has used at least three definitions, which they cite as follows: "1.) the preservation of the rights of individuals, 2.) a universal mode of choosing, and 3.) respect for persons."[11] Regardless of how justice is to be defined, Hall and Davis think that Kohlberg is wrong to view it as the exclusive core of morality. They are not the only ones, of course, who have taken this position. There are other principles which could be identified as possessing universal scope, such as liberty, which could serve as the loadstone for autonomous stage 6 moral reasoning. Even if one were to confine the stage 6 moral vision to justice, there is a remarkably small amount of cross-cultural agreement on its meaning, which Simpson, in "Moral Development Research," has pointed out. Diverse cultures conceive of justice differently, which places its universal status in jeopardy. Hall and Davis do not agree with Kohlberg that "respect for persons" is a pure principle constituting only the form of a mode of thought. It has a distinctively substantive character which can be compared, for example, to respect for law. While they reject justice as the core and exclusive principle of morality, they do adopt a version of an autonomous stage 6 individual who is principled in his moral reasoning.

The value of life has been given a position of supremacy over all other values in the Kohlbergian scheme. This is repeatedly brought out in most of Kohlberg's writings. The vehicle for highlighting this supreme value is the classic story of Heinz, told in chapter 4, in which a husband (Heinz) is tempted to steal a drug from the local pharamacist to save his wife from dying of cancer. The pharmacist, who has discovered the drug, is asking an exorbitant amount, which Heinz cannot possibly afford. In each context that Kohlberg discusses this dilemma, he makes it abundantly clear that the moral thing to do is for Heniz to steal the drug in order to save the life of his wife. The rationale is the sovereignty of life over all other values, certainly including property. Simpson has leveled a serious challenge to Kohlberg's claim to the universality and priority of this principle. She explores diverse cultural attitudes about this matter and concludes that the issue is not one of valuing life over all other values, but rather ". . . *that it is valued situationally in highly culturally-specific ways.*" [12] In one culture a traitor will be killed; in another a person may be killed to protect him or her from what others might do; and in another the elderly are left to die. The Congress of the United States has sent millions off to war, knowing that hordes of them would die; the wars were not always just. Patrick Henry has said, "Give me liberty, or give me death." Simpson reminds us that after losing property in the Great Depression, men jumped off buildings and put bullets through their head. She states:

> History is full of examples of men and women who have freely given of their lives for the preservation of their own property or the property of others. The point is that the relative value of property and life is decided situationally and culturally and is not a matter of natural and universal knowledge.[13]

Returning to the Heinz dilemma itself, one may wonder about its particular construction and the implication of Kohlberg's position. Kohlberg has designed the story in such a way that the pharmacist is a villian. A greedy capitalist, we might say. But why has he done this? The fact that the druggist is charging a grossly excessive amount is actually a contaminant in the situation which is entirely unnecessary if the principle is a valid guide to action. Kohlberg could have had the druggist asking only what it might reasonably cost under the circumstances. He did invent the drug, after all, and it might well be a scarce commodity. It is entirely conceivable that Heinz may still not be able to afford the drug. However, we all know that it is much easier to steal from a bad guy than a good guy. Hence, the story calls for the druggist insisting upon the exorbitant cost. If there is any conflict for our moral reasoner between advocating that Heinz break the law and save his wife versus maintaining the law and allowing his wife to die, Kohlberg's story construction will help to tip the scale for him. Furthermore, an elaboration of the story can certainly bring to light situational variables that might modify the response. If the drug is scarce, does stealing it mean that another person in need will die because of the theft? At what cost to himself has the druggist invented the drug? He may hypothetically have isolated himself for many years and worked arduously to discover this drug, at great personal sacrifice. If so, how is a just price to be placed upon it? Under these conditions, the mere theft of the drug is actually depriving the druggist of more than a piece of property. Has the druggist worked hard to discover the drug in order to sell it for a large sum so that he would then have the money that *he* needs to order an operation for his own debilitated wife? If so, is it right for Heinz to steal the drug? True, these are all hypothetical possibilities, but they are conceivable and they do have a bearing on the morality of the judgment. Furthermore, how does Heinz know whether any of these possibilities obtain? Most likely he does not; but he can know, if he pauses to think about it, that they might possibly obtain. How is this meta-reflection to modify the judgment one is to make about the dilemma?

Kohlberg further suggests two significant ideas regarding morality in the Heinz situation. One is that Heinz should steal the drug even if the woman is a stranger to him and the other is that it is not only right for Heinz if he does steal, but it is wrong if he does not. The first of these is consistent with the universality of the principle upon which the action is to be predicated. The second has to do with reciprocal rights and obligations. If Heinz has the right to expect that someone should steal to save his life, should the tables be turned, then he has the obligation to steal for another in the same situation. The paradox, however, is that if our moral reasoner is at stage 6, he will surely find his intellect taking him far beyond the concrete situation to the many possibilities of human suffering and life-endangering situations throughout the world. He *knows* that dying people can use his physical and financial aid. There is no justification for being rooted in the present situation. There are literally millions of strangers in the world whom Heinz can be sacrificing for. He may even actually save the lives of one or two. Interpreting the valuing of life as Kohlberg does, it is difficult to see how any fully principled stage 6 moral reasoner can justify his own existence as long as his possessions are in excess of a subsistence level allowing mere survival. Any excess beyond what is needed for survival may be defined as property which can be used to save the lives of others. If the value of life is to be interpreted as a pure universal principle, superordinate over all other values regardless of circumstances, then the moral obligation is to yield what one owns in excess of what he must have to survive.

Looking at the problem from a different perspective, suppose a family has three children. One is in the second year of college and another is about to start. A third, tragically, is dying. The family physician and two outside consultants, both experts in the field of the child's disease, insist that at best the child can be kept alive in the hospital for six more months through the use of extraordinary means. By hypothesis, maintaining him there would completely wipe out the family savings, accumulated over many hardworking years. The savings were intended to be used for the children's college. At stage 6 would it be moral to choose not to prolong the life of the child after weighing the six months' gain against the probable total loss of the money and what it would purchase in terms of humanistic values for the two remaining children? Consistency with Kohlberg's principle as a superordinate absolute would dictate keeping the child alive. Yet I believe that while doing so is a perfectly viable stage 6 choice, so is the alternative, even thought the choice would not be to maintain life at *any* cost. Death is inevitable. To seek to maintain life at *all* costs, despite circumstances, can be compulsively destructive. Imagine that death never occurs and there is no technology allowing escape to other planets. Overpopulation would eventually reach the point of so diminishing the quality of life that existence would become insufferable. I believe that a rational person would design a world in which life would be time-limited, hence permitting all to enjoy a higher quality of it during the finite period of living. Thus it follows that given the imaginative possibility to enshrine life as a sovereign principle that will endure everlastingly, the rational person will reject the opportunity and opt for a society in which each member will eventually experience death; himself included, as that would only be fair. It would appear that this choice must imply values other and higher than the mere sustainment of life. I would argue that those values are based on a "respect for persons" every bit as much as the Kohlbergian interpretation of the "value of life." When death is occurring naturally and the ordinary resources for preventing it, which at best in all cases can only mean forestalling it, are not available, then it is not unethical to allow it to occur. Further, one is not obliged at great personal loss to attempt to prevent it. Undoubtedly, if the third child in the dilemma above could be not simply saved for six months, but could recover at the expense of the family savings, then there would be no dilemma, for the course of action would be obvious. Supposing, however, the dying child lives next door and belongs to another family. Would the first family be morally obliged to give up all of its savings for the sake of helping the child next door to recover? The universal principle would dictate that it would be so obliged, just as it would be if the child were a stranger from across the world whose parents suddenly knocked at the door. Theoretically implicit in Kohlberg's position is the premise that an individual must virtually be enslaved to another, as long as that other is in need of the first person's income to keep alive. To concede otherwise is to acknowledge that the sanctity of one person's life does not always take precedent over the property of another person. However, this is exactly what Kohlberg does not seem to acknowledge in his many philosophical tracts. I cannot help wondering if Kohlberg has thought through all of the ramifications of the microcosmic Heinz story and if he has, whether he is willing to claim them. In my opinion, however, the truly autonomous stage 6 person would not give a narrowly confined response, whatever his ultimate recommendation, to the Heinz dilemma. Precisely because of his sociocognitive moral maturity he would be compelled to entertain alternate possibilities that might obtain in the situation and to anticipate the reverberating implications of his decision from many perspectives. To the extent that Kohlberg maintains a purity and singularity of definition, viewing justice as a *mode of choosing,* there is no disagreement. It is clear, however, that Kohlberg sees a converging of form and content at stage 6 and that he seeks to impose his own ideological content at that point. The distinction between form and content in moral reasoning is compromised by its own maker.

Now let us move a step beyond Kohlberg. I have tried to show that it is not necessarily *just* to view an individual as obliged to offer up all of his property and continuing income, in excess of his survival needs, to save other people from a natural death, which is inevitable at some time in any event. But what if an individual volitionally chooses to do so? Supposing the family members living next door to the dying child confer and all agree to sacrifice their savings and forgo college, at least in the present, for the children. Have they not made a moral choice that goes beyond justice into the realm of love. Certainly they value the life of the dying child, but their choice is not made out of a cognitive sense of correlative rights and duties; instead, it is generated by a mature form of brotherhood and love. It moves away from egocentricity and toward universality since the child is not in their own family. If they were to make the same sacrifice for a child who is a stranger to them, then their choice would be based on love that has become completely universalized. It is an irony of the world's religions that many of them have impeded the universalization of love. Contrary to their own doctrines, many churches throughout history have created among their membership a divisive feeling between themselves as insiders and others as outsiders. Love is reserved for the insiders and withheld from the outsiders. Of course, love as morality is not what Kohlberg is talking about. The question, however, is whether justice as morality is not an arbitrary and unnecessarily delimiting conception.

Puka, in "Moral Education and Its Cure," repudiates justice entirely as the core of morality, reconstruing it as a political concept. Morality itself encompasses a broader framework, within which justice orients us to what we cannot eliminate doing and must refrain from doing, in order that we not fall into the class of immoral. Because of this emphasis, it is seen as the negative side of morality. The positive side of morality places the concept of "better" at its center. It functions not to resolve conflicts, but to promote the growth of individuals. Puka sees the goal as becoming better people, so that we evolve to a moral consciousness that brings us to ". . . the transcendence of judgmentalism, obligation, duty, rights, blame, guilt, censure, and even justifiable resentment."[14] In a deontological theory, one does the right thing because duty commands it. The stage 6 person anticipates that if he doesn't act upon what he knows to be right, then he will have violated his self-ideal and will experience self-inflicted negative sanctions. In a positive morality, people have developed socially so that they genuinely want to do what they perceive as what they ought to do. Ideals and self-interests coincide.

Although a just decision-making procedure may satisfy the demands of Kohlberg's concept of morality, it is entirely conceivable that a fair compromise solution to a conflict may not satisfy the actual participants themselves. Puka questions whether, in fact, it is justice and satisfaction they should be in pursuit of. He introduces the intriguing notion that a positive morality utilizing a love ethic may neutralize a conflict and offer a resolution that transcends justice. As an example he cites the famous lifeboat dilemma in which several survivors of a shipwreck stand a chance to survive only if two people leave the raft to face certain death. The rational stage 6 just solution calls for drawing straws to determine who shall go overboard. However, he conveys that at a conference on moral development which he attended, the discussants simulating being in this dilemma agreed not to draw straws, but to take their chances with one another instead. The likelihood of survival with all aboard would be slim. Puka urges that the choice made reflects a love ethic which is higher and nobler than a morality of justice. There was, however, one dissenting participant who argued that the decision of the others was unfair and might be responsible for his possible death. Puka agrees that when considered in the abstract, the dissenter was justified, even though all of the others made an opposite choice when role-playing the situation with great feeling. The name of the dissenter, incidentally, was Lawrence Kohlberg.

The lifeboat dilemma could be complicated by first assuming that there are four survivors, all of whom agree to draw straws. Once the straws have been drawn, the two who lose refuse to jump overboard. We may further assume hypothetically that had the other two lost, they would have kept the contract. That would, of course, have been unfair to them because, although they would not have known it, they stood to lose to some extent either way. However, they now do know where they stand and are faced with the two who have reneged on the bargain. Is it *just* for them to overpower the losers and throw them overboard? Does it involve a higher morality to see the losers' behavior as based upon fear of certain death, rather than viciousness, and to embrace them as brothers without resentment?

A final perspective in this chapter exploring criticisms of Kohlberg is drawn from "In a Different Voice," by Gilligan, who refutes the tendency in developmental moral psychology to view women as in some way deficient. No longer willing to accept the males' independence and commitment to the work world, with its emphasis upon responsible decision-making, as superior to the contextual, caring, interpersonal focus of women, Gilligan speaks for the distinctively female voice. The alleged deficiency in women's moral development is reinterpreted as actually representative of an equal type of social and moral concern. Both Freud and Kohlberg are noted as viewing women's morality as lower on the developmental scale than that of men. In particular, Kohlberg found that women, given their strong interpersonal orientation, favored stage 3 in development, a stage he claims to be both functional and adequate for them. Gilligan comments incisively in a way that commands one to reflect seriously upon the matter, as she states:

> And yet, herein lies the paradox, for the very traits that have traditionally defined the "goodness" of women, their care for and sensitivity to the needs of others, are those that mark them as deficient in moral development. The infusion of feeling into their judgments keeps them from developing a more independent and abstract ethical conception in which concern for others derives from principles of justice rather than from compassion and care.[15]

Gilligan joins Haan ("Activism As Moral Protest") and Holstein ("Development of Moral Judgment") in suggesting that Kohlberg's scoring system may be based on a standard that is biased against women. It is not the varying qualitative structures that are brought into question, but the subordination of the interpersonal orientation to that of the conventional definition of good that is maintained by the society. She stresses the disproportionate number of males and adolescents to be found in research samples and the fact that the underlying developmental theories tend to be formulated by males. This results in a departure from the male standard being viewed as inferior. The research of Haan and Holstein points up divergences between men and women. The women appear to express greater concern for dilemmas reflecting real situations that one is more likely to encounter. Empathy and compassion are more typical of them than of the men, who lean in the direction of being more concerned with that which deals with the hypothetical. The central dilemma for women developmentally, as seen by Gilligan, derives from the traditional feminine notion of the good as self-sacrifice. The female's problem in attaining adulthood without losing what is valued in her femininity is to resolve the struggle between self and other. As Gilligan puts it, "It is precisely this dilemma—the conflict between compassion and autonomy, between virtue and power—which the feminine voice struggles to resolve in its effort to reclaim the self and to solve the moral problem in such a way that no one is hurt."[16] To sharpen the true and genuinely female developmental moral process, Gilligan selected to do research with women engaged in choosing a course of action revolving around the possibility of abortion. It is a problem exquisitely suited for her purposes. The women are in a condition which is specifically feminine and there is no alternative to their making an active choice, one for which they must assume responsibility, regardless of what it is. The tendency of so many women in society to be passive and not actively choose would not be possible in this situation. Although her own self-interests must be taken into account, the choice will impact upon others. Therefore, the typical female motive to avoid hurting others may come into conflict with pursuing the interests of her own self.

In listening to the women exploring their feelings and concerns, Gilligan identified a distinctively "feminine voice," a language focusing upon the need to evidence care for others and to avoid hurting them. The latter is based on a commitment not to be selfish and the former is conceived of as expressing responsibility. To hurt another is to be immoral; to demonstrate caring is to be moral. The mature adult, male or female, must integrate into his or her moral vision both care and compassion for others. Certainly these "feminine" characteristics are as worthy of universalization in a fully-developed moral system as the independent, decision-making, autonomous self of Kohlberg's male-oriented scheme. Gilligan suggests that the emphasis upon separation and independent judgment so prevalent in some of Kohlberg's more mature subjects is actually a reflection of their adolescent struggles. To become fully mature, those qualities must be integrated with the feminine voice. It is only upon the advent of a successful synthesis that true adulthood is reached for either male or female. The self must become capable of both separation and connection with others.

The women Gilligan found to be at the highest level identified a principle of responsibility for self and others as distinguished from Kohlberg's emphasis upon rights and duties. She is critical of his moral dilemma stories because they are designed in a fashion that removes them from the real-live social context. When reconstructed and embedded in that context, the causes and consequences of the moral decision making are manifest. The Kohlberg stories work to the disadvantage of the female, whose special moral strengths are accentuated by the type of reconstructed story design Gilligan refers to. She notes that the women in her research, who were given three of Kohlberg's moral dilemmas, had a tendency to embellish and restructure the stories so that they did not respond in the abstract in terms of rights and duties. Instead they sought more information about the circumstances and explored the stories from the standpoint of who would be hurt and what would the consequences be to the participants of alternate choices. Gilligan finds that many of the responses given by her subjects do not fit the Kohlbergian stages and, therefore, are not readily scorable. She believes that the male-biased research sample from which the stages have emerged accounts specifically for a frame of reference which is different from that which women bring to the moral dilemmas. Viewing the Heinz dilemma from the perspective of not wanting to hurt, one woman began to recast the dilemma in terms of societal institutions that permit exploitation. Another stressed how, regardless of the choice Heinz might make, he would suffer guilt and his life would be sundered from his wife's. She would either die or he would most likely wind up going to jail. Gilligan pinpoints women's characteristic ways of responding to the dilemma in the following remark: "When women begin to make direct moral statements, the issues they repeatedly address are those of exploitation and hurt."[17] At the principled level, they adopt a moral world view that is based upon a structural comprehension of non-violence, which facilitates their attempt at establishing justice when encountering moral conflicts. This is markedly different from the male proclivity to respond by searching for abstract principles pivoting around rights and obligations. Gilligan points out the potential danger in a formalized ethical system which unyieldingly seeks to impose sovereign principles upon the real world at the cost of suffering to people.

Summing up her critical stance on Kohlberg, she comments as follows: "Kohlberg's research on moral development has confounded the variables of age, sex, type of decision, and type of dilemma by presenting a single configuration (the responses of adolescent males to hypothetical dilemmas of conflicting rights) as the basis for a universal stage sequence."[18]

Gilligan has opened up new vistas in understanding feminine moral development. Beyond that, however, she has discovered the missing piece which Kohlberg's autonomous man must integrate if he is to progress to adult moral maturity.

As with any significant philosophical thought or scientific endeavor, Kohlberg's cognitive-structural theory of moral development has been the target of a considerable body of critical commentary. It has been sternly criticized on both methodological and theoretical grounds. There are those who argue that despite Kohlberg's claims to the contrary, the invariant sequence and cross-cultural universality of the theory have not been proven. Others have criticized the selection of justice as the central concept of morality for being arbitrary and unduly restrictive. Still others would seek to reinstate affect, habit, trait, and a concern for others to their proper place in a comprehensive system of moral psychology. The charge of sex bias in the methodology has been leveled from some quarters, while the soundness of the research technology utilized by Kohlberg and his collaborators has been questioned elsewhere.

I have been purposefully unsparing in presenting the criticism that Kohlberg's work has drawn. To avoid diluting its impact, I have not attempted a point-by-point rebuttal. In a very real sense, except for this chapter and the one that follows, this book is itself a response to much of the criticism. As time goes on, some of the criticism becomes outdated. Some of it is based on misconceptions of Kohlberg's work specifically, and some derives from a lack of congeniality toward the congitive-developmental approach generally. Nevertheless, a portion of the criticism certainly has merit and must be answered by Kohlberg (see his "Cognitive-Developmental Approach") if he is to continue to develop his theory toward the highest stage of theoretical adequacy that is possible in the field of sociomoral knowledge.

On balance, in my judgment, Kohlberg's theory and research establish an essentially accurate formulation of moral development. At the same time, the body of extant criticism urges that one recognize limitations in the Kohlbergian model. Acknowledging these limitations, let us go on to explore the model's utility.

# Chapter Seven

## Concepts and Strategies
## for Intervention

Neither Piaget nor Kohlberg had set out to deliver theory or techniques for practice to the helping professions. Yet it was inevitable
that the cognitive-structural approach to development would generate new ways of conceiving practice and action models for carrying
them out. There does not exist a single monolithic technique for
guiding all practice, but instead a diversity of ideas for application has
gradually been emerging from several related sources, all deriving
from a sociocognitive or moral developmental paradigm. The present
chapter is designed to introduce some of the most suggestive and
promising attempts at applying those ideas that have appeared thus
far. In presenting this material I have classified each of the approaches under one of three perspectives: the psychodynamic, the interpersonal, and the organizational. There is no doubt that in each
case an argument could be made for classifying a particular approach
under another category. The distinctions are a matter of emphasis
and sometimes subtle. Nevertheless, I have adopted this formulation
in the hope that it will impart at least a shade more of understanding
as the reader encounters the material.

Kegan has been classified under the psychodynamic perspective
both because that seems to be his own preference and because of the
special phenomenological focus his work reflects in discussing the
developing person. Abroms is viewed within an interpersonal matrix
because of the emphasis he gives to the dialectic between the therapist's developmental stage and that of the client. Selman and Chan-

dler are also both classified under the interpersonal perspective and this is so because of the attention they pay to promoting the ability to see the other person's viewpoint and the effect this has on one's relationships and interpersonal behavior. Lastly, because the intervention by Kohlberg and his collaborators is explicitly intended to affect the climate and structure of organizations such as schools and prisons, their work is presented within the organizational perspective.

## THE PSYCHODYNAMIC PERSPECTIVE

In "Ego and Truth," Kegan has attempted to elaborate upon the Piagetian system, integrating affective components, to emerge with an impressive and striking theory of personality. The central concept which proves to be the key to unlocking a comprehensive personality theory from the system is equilibration. The equilibrating process that undergirds an ongoing activity in which the self is taken through a progression of self-other disengaging and rebalancing stages is the major theme winding through Kegan's extensions of Piaget and Kohlberg. Equilibration as seen from the outside is descriptive of the cognitive aspect, but the "self-constituting meaning making" constituent of equilibration is the phenomenological feeling aspect. Kegan, in his formulation, feels that his approach is an interactionist one, escaping a mere intrapsychic focus. Consider his rather bold statement:

> Each re-equilibration of a person's self-other balance brings the equilibrative whole into greater balance, and—outrageous as it must sound—changes the world. The importance of saying so is to stress that such transformation does not go on only in someone's head, but means something to the balance of the universe, and most immediately to those persons and social organizations which people that individual's other.[1]

The helper who concentrates upon facilitating the equilibrating process in the individual will of necessity be involved in the social matrix. Further, the helper must assume a responsibility for considering the manner in which the "others" of his client might be affected by further development in the client.

The work of Kegan is profound and comprehensive. I plan to introduce only two facets of it here beyond the preceding introductory remarks. The first is an alternate way of conceptualizing depression, which differs from the standardized approach of diagnostic and descriptive psychiatry. It is based upon a study by Kegan of thirty-nine cases and is linked to Kohlberg's stage theory. I will then follow with some of Kegan's general comments on the significance of a cognitive-structural approach for the helper.

Kegan investigated the data that had been accumulated on each of the thirty-nine patients in his study. He had access to staff reports, intake information, material describing interpersonal relationships and social milieu, and the patients' descriptive formulations of their own condition. He discerned an underlying pattern which he organized into three discrete categories reflecting the world view of the individuals involved. Kegan chose the affect of depression around which the three classifications were galvanized. Some of the patients were clinically depressed, but others were not. His use of depression, however, was independent of the patients' official psychiatric diagnosis. Instead he viewed it as an emotional state of varying intensities which was found to one degree or another in all of the patients. A patient so viewed was not necessarily found to be depressed all of the time or with great intensity. Because the Kohlberg instrument is fairly tuned to measuring the state of balance between self and other, Kegan's central developmental interest, he adopted it as a theoretical framework. He found that each of the three categories reflecting patients' views of their world reality bore a strong relationship to one of three Kohlbergian stages, as interpreted by Kegan himself. Furthermore, their stages did not correlate with their diagnoses as determined with the use of standard psychiatric nomenclature. In other words, no particular stage was more frequently associated with either neurosis or psychosis. Similarly, for example, no one Kohlbergian stage was more readily associated with a specific psychotic state or with a character-disordered personality. Thus, persons found to be within a particular Kohlbergian group could be from any one of the standard psychiatric categories, but they held in common a phenomenological outlook about their world reality. Briefly, despite having been labeled variously from a psychiatric standpoint, they had constructed a certain way of knowing the world which they shared. In this study, that shared feature which earned them membership in a Kohlbergian group was typified by a characteristic form of a depressive affect. Kegan, in effect, is maintaining that this reconceptualization of emotionally disturbed people provides a new way of understanding them through their own phenomenology based upon qualitatively different ways of knowing-in-the-world.

The first kind of depression identified by Kegan is referred to as "self-sacrificing."[2] It revolves around the subject's own needs. Each of the three types has a fundamental concern. The concern for the self-sacrificing type is the discontinuance of need gratification. An alternative concern of this type, should needs be met, is the mounting cost to the individual of having his needs met. There is an uneasy anticipation that should need satisfaction not be achieved, the *I* of the subject will cease to be.

The second kind of depression has as its main concern the interpersonal context with the accompanying potential for loss of relationships. Subjects experiencing this variation of the affect feel helpless, hopeless, weak, and lonely. They are especially sensitive to the threat of being abandoned. Subjects in this phenomenological category, called "dependent depression," are preoccupied with the apprehension they have over angering or hurting others. There exists an overriding fear that should a significant relationship terminate, the *I* of the subject will disappear along with it.

The third kind of depression expresses concern over an incapacity to execute one's proper role, conceived independently of others' judgments, and to live up to one's own standards. The world is experienced as a meaningless void. Guilt and despair are prevalent feelings. Kegan calls this "guilty depression." It is feared that faced with a lack of role fulfillment and failure to appropriately discharge responsibilities, the *I* will evaporate.

In each case, apart from the threat of annihilation of self, there is also the overriding apprehension that the basic orientation implied in the outlook is without meaning. For example, in dependent depression there is an underlying fear that an interpersonal outlook in life as a source of meaning and security may itself be without any foundation. Kegan observed a stability within each patient, such that an individual subject consistently reflected the same orientation and did not shift from one to another.

Upon invoking the Kohlberg measure, it was found that a strong association existed between self-sacrificing, dependent, and guilty forms of depression with stages 2 or 2–3 transitional, 3 or 3–4 transitional, and 4 or 4–5 transitional, respectively. Approximately half of the patients were scored in the transitional state. By transitional, Kegan is not alluding merely to stage mixture. It is a state in which the subject possesses a unitary outlook which has passed beyond one stage, but has not yet achieved a new balance or centration typical of the following stage. Hence, a transitional state is said to be characterized by a single world-view of its own, existing midway between the perspectives of two balanced stages. The subject in transition may hold a critical attitude toward the balanced stage from which he is moving away, while not yet exhibiting the rebalanced perspective to be acquired at the stage he is moving toward. An alternate criterion for assigning a subject to a transitional phase is finding him to be undergoing the dissonance of simultaneously experiencing the perspectives of two consecutive stages. Kegan points out that while transition entails previous disequilibria, not all stages of disequilibrium necessarily signify further transition. Kegan makes many subtle, complex, and sometimes even abstruse distinctions. His work is bold and innovative. He is attempting to be not simply a Piagetian "cognitivist" but "psychodynamicist." I will not be quite as bold, and so will refrain from pursuing his work through every compartment of the labyrnth he has constructed. However, I would like to trace his efforts just a few more steps.

Kegan conceptualizes depression as being more a matter of disequilibrium, in his terms, than transition. The Kohlberg measure picks up the features of transition, but not disequilibrium in the psychodynamic sense. Kegan is in full accord with the cognitive emphasis that depression will be known variously, contingent upon stage of development. He states:

> The correlation I have just reported is not by itself evidence that depression is related to *disequilibrium*. It *is* evidence that when people are depressed they will describe, construe, and probably experience, their depression in different ways depending on ego level. It is evidence that a "feeling" is known differently at different "levels of knowing." [3]

Kegan, however, is struggling to establish more than the above, which reflects a purely cognitive interpretation. In striving to go beyond the cognitive, he conceptualizes what he views as the psychodynamic interpretation that would flow from a Piagetian and Kohlbergian orientation. He goes on to observe:

> But what I am suggesting is that depression . . . *is not only shaped but is about that shaping activity.* Our hypothesis is not that, once depressed, meaning-constitutive activity will cast a meaning for this experience as it will for any others; but that depression is meaning-constitution itself under assault. Meaning-constitution, in equilibrium, is a matter, not

of an individual's *having* an "answer" for the world, but of an individual's *being* an "answer." Yet those "depression concerns" . . . are not . . . mere grist for the "answer" that is equilibrium; rather they express the particular forms by which meaning-constitution in disequilibrium leaves the individual, not so much *having* a "question," as *being* one.[4]

Kegan's own meaning in this somewhat opaque quote is difficult to grasp. He is, first of all, going beyond a cognitive-structural position which would assert that the stage of cognitive development in an individual structures the way he interprets the depression he may experience. In that viewpoint, cognitive stage is the independent variable and depression is the dependent variable. I have indicated above that Kegan does not reject such a position. However, his psychodynamic reformulation introduces an existential quality not evident in the original formulation. For Kegan, the core of depression is itself one form or another of radical doubt about the very foundation of what ordinarily constitutes meaning at a given developmental stage. It might be said that at such a point one's existence is in essence meaning that has become undermined and challenged. Hence, the individual is not simply asking a question, but is experiencing his very existence as questionable.

Kegan reasons that a constructive-developmentalist views growth as going from stages of diminishing subjectivity to increasing objectivity. Development moves away from self-contradictory and less adequate subjectivity toward that which is more equilibrated in that it more adequately covers a wider range of situations and demands. Progressively, development is the construction of a world-view that is "true-for-all." The rebalance between self and other at a given stage is more adequate than the preceding balance. At stage 2, the subject is emmeshed in his own needs, hence loss of satisfaction of those needs constitutes loss of self. The shift from stage 2 to 3 entails a decentering from one's own needs. The self must no longer be equated with its needs. Instead the subject will go on to experience the self as that which possesses needs, but is not the same as them. The self, no longer exclusively embedded in the own needs, may reflect upon them in stage 3. The needs of other people are clearly recognized and at stage 3 are coordinated with one's own needs. Because of this shift there has occurred a rebalancing of self and other which has a defining characteristic of an interpersonal matrix. Prior to transition, while still at stage 2, there is an assimilation of events and potential precipitants of change to that stage. There occurs little in the way of accommodation, with the result that the scope of experience that is realistically adapted to is severely limited. Kegan refers to the person in such a fixed state, regardless of stage, as a "balance defender." Each new rebalancing of self and other allows for an enlarged range of adaptive experience, although it is characterized by limitations in relation to the following stages. Before achieving a rebalanced state there is a phase of disequilibrium during which there is a sense of having lost one self without having acquired a new self. The epistemic subject, in going from stage 2 to 3, is unaware that his needs per se are not being lost, but rather that he is giving up a way of conceiving them for a more adequate orientation. The person who suffers depression as a result of this kind of concern is experiencing "radical doubt" about the continued existence of self.

In discussing clinical case material of a fifteen-year-old female on a hospital ward, Kegan asserted that an insight-oriented treatment would be contraindicated for a patient not yet at stage 3. The patient saw others merely as thwarting the fulfillment of her needs. On the ward she was seen by staff as resistant and manipulative in that she appeared more interested in finding out what she was supposed to say, rather than genuinely sharing something of her self. She did not experience guilt, but was concerned over whether her mother would learn that she had lied pertaining to a certain matter. Her problems were viewed by her as having their locus in the external environment. The staff react to her with distaste. Kegan suggests a reconceptualization which takes some of the onus off the patient and may even perhaps lead to more accepting attitudes by staff, as well as to a more effective treatment strategy. Taking a constructive-developmentalist position, Kegan points out the patient's mode of being is consistent with a stage 2 orientation. By locating the source of difficulty for herself as external, she is reflecting a developmental stage. It is as "true" for her that the difficulties she is experiencing have an external locus as it would be that the person at a later stage who talks of guilt experiences his difficulties as internal. The patient is not being resistant in the sense of concealing a deeper self which she guardedly refuses to unveil. By her statements and actions she is revealing, in fact, the self that there is. Labeling her as a "sociopath," which the hospital did, is not a particularly helpful step, with the pejorative implications that such a label carries, as do many other

labels. Rather than viewing the patient as having a psychiatric ill-
ness, Kegan's approach would suggest an equilibrative analysis with
a view toward promoting development to a more adequate stage. The
particular patient in this case was bound to frustrate the staff, which
could hardly be helpful to the patient, because she was expected to
meet the demands of hospital milieu treatment. Yet that treatment
approach requires that a participating patient have at least a Stage 3
interpersonal orientation. The stage 2 patient is not "acting out" or
being willfully resistant, for such a patient truly does not as yet have
a way of "knowing" the requirements of the treatment contract.

Kegan makes the intriguing suggestion that the precipitating
events leading to hospitalization may vary according to stages. That
is, a specific type or range of events may account for hospitalization
of those patients at one stage and these precipitants may differ for patients at another stage. It is those events which an individual at a particular stage can neither assimilate nor accommodate, which cannot
be meaningfully ordered and adapted to by his world-view, that
would result in disequilibrium sufficiently severe as to warrant hospitalization. One thing that is clear from Kegan's groundbreaking work
is that the concept of equilibration is utilized to explain much more
than Piaget's cognitive periods, and that the stage theory of Kohlberg
opens a door to understanding much wider aspects of personality
than moral development only. The equilibrative analysis brought to
bear upon the young patient at stage 2 is merely an example of what
may be done with any person regardless of developmental position. It
is the equilibration process which is at the heart of Kegan's conception of personality drawn from the work of Piaget and Kohlberg. Each
stage is a way station of dynamic stability along the path of the self-
other reequilibrating process toward greater objectivity. The role of
the helping person then, in a constructive-developmental viewpoint,
is to facilitate the equilibrating activity. More adaptive ways of
knowing-in-the-world is the pivotal point of growth. Knowledge is not
dormant, waiting within the individual to be uncovered or activated.
Knowledge is constructed developmentally as the epistemic subject
experiences dissonance upon encountering events he cannot adequately construe. The knowing subject must resolve the discrepancy
between his present meaning system and the unassimilatible event
by constituting meaning anew. Despite the phenomenological emphasis in Kegan's work, he avoids the pure existentialist position

which honors the uniqueness of each person's meaning system accompanied by a refusal to acknowledge objective meaning in the world. He believes strongly, as I do, that one may respect the uniqueness of the individual, without according parity to all of his specific convictions.

The helping person shares with the helpee the very process that the former seeks to stimulate in the latter. The helper is engaged in his own developmental process just as is the helpee. Kegan reformulates conventional ways of looking at the helping process when he states that the way he looks at the helpee:

> . . . derives not from convictions about "patients" or "sick persons" or even "persons with problems," or "persons in pain," but simply (and complexly) about persons growing. Hence, the clinician's most fundamental orientation toward the persons with whom he works derives from convictions about an activity he shares *at that very moment* with the persons with whom he works. . . . We neither escape from our own fate as life-long meaning-makers nor escape from our life-long fraternity or peoplehood with those who may be finding that fate a greater burden.[5]

I believe that this formulation of the helping process diminishes its hierarchical character and links both helper and helpee in a mutual growth process.

## THE INTERPERSONAL PERSPECTIVE

### Psychotherapy as Value Change

In "The Place of Values in Psychotherapy," Abroms, in a similar vein to Kegan, but concentrating upon a narrower scope, has argued that while the therapist cannot impose his own personal and narcissistic goals upon the client or patient, he should derive power and direction from the transpersonal values he embraces. It is those higher-order values which the therapist must move the patient toward. The therapist, just as he does not impose his purely subjective interests, also does not mindlessly help the patient to achieve any goal regardless of how narcissistically and selfishly determined it may be. Abroms sees psychotherapy as a process of value change primarily and symptomatic relief as only a secondary component. To achieve the goal of assisting the patient toward adopting higher-order values, the therapist must, himself, be at a higher level than the patient. Abroms envisions the therapist as the embodiment of inspirational ideals held forth before the patient. He has adopted Kohlberg's stage theory of moral development because it is his conviction that it can become a loadstone which provides guidance in selecting appropriate treatment goals and methods.

At stage 1, the aim of therapy is to assure physical and material well-being. The keynote at this stage is sheer survival. Treatment methods correspond to biomedical methods and conditioned learning theory. Stage 2 rises above an embeddedness in sheer survival needs to encompass pleasure seeking. Activities which have a survival function, such as eating and sex, may be engaged in for pure pleasure. Treatment seeks to facilitate appropriately uninhibited expressiveness and to reward pleasure. Although Abroms is not specific in differentiating among the many varieties of behavior therapy, it would seem that positive reinforcement would be appropriate at both stages 1 and 2, but with different aims in mind. Punishment, in technical learning theory terms, might best be reserved for stage 1, as in the use of aversive therapy to prevent an autistic child from continuing to batter his head against the wall. It should be noted that Abroms himself does not explicitly recommend this. The use of aversive therapy to treat any problem has been ruled out by some ethicists. Others, however, would argue that it is the only alternative to certain death or brain damage in some cases.

Treatment methods at stage 3 have a socializing goal, regardless of whether individual, group, or family modalities are brought to bear. The necessity for survival and desirability of pleasure are not eliminated, but are subordinated to the value of belonging and socialization. At stage 4, the orderliness of the total social unit going beyond one's personal social matrix is recognized. Hence therapy seeks to institute ego controls and a sanctification of proper authority. There is a valuing of rule-regulating behavior to which the self is subordinated. The maintenance of order goes beyond the mere seeking of approval within the sphere of one's personal society of significant others.

At stage 5 one is no longer rigidly bound by the preexisting laws of the land. One is capable of creatively innovating new laws and institutional arrangements to seek a higher justice than the prevailing one. Adaptive flexibility is said to be the chief mental health value. Abroms holds that at this stage the formation of utilitarian contracts becomes a matter that should receive paramount attention in the therapy, with a special emphasis upon the commitment to adhere to those contracts consented to. At stage 6 universal values assume a role of supremacy over the relativity inherent in adaptive flexibility. Therapy now seeks "The synthesis of a cohesive self with an idealized super-ego, devoted to the realization of social justice. . . ."[6]

Abroms elaborates at some length upon the relative fit between developmental level and therapist. It is out of the dialectical process between the two that development to the next stage in the hierarchy can occur. The essential point, however, is that the therapist must be at least one stage above the patient in his own personal development, if he is to facilitate the patient's growth. If he is merely at or below the patient's dominant stage, then failure in the therapeutic endeavor is inevitable. The problem of mismatch can occur at the other end of the scale, as when a therapist, at a stage much higher than the patient, will offer interpretations at a level beyond what the patient can possibly comprehend. In such a case, the patient will either reject the lofty wisdom or assimilate it to a mode of comprehension that depletes its potentially meaningful contribution. Hence, Abroms advances a view of therapeutic competence in which:

> One aspect of technical skill involves the ability to exemplify health and personal values at a level appropriate to the client's sophistication in cognitive and moral awareness. The therapist cannot, for example, interpret troublesome behavior as lacking in fairness or loyalty if the client is a devoted hedonist, out for his own pleasure and uncomprehending of the rejection that he thereby provokes. According to the schema, the technically appropriate intervention would involve interpretations and corrective experiences aimed at the issues of social concordance (Stage 3) or the organizational and personal boundaries (Stage 4) that he has violated.[7]

Technical competence, in Abroms's view, would direct the therapist to formulate an interpretation or promote discussion at stage 3 for the stage 2 hedonist. The focus of communication would be upon the social unit confined to the patient's personalized experiences and significant others. This could encompass the immediate family, circle of friends, or organizational milieu. The impact of the patient's behavior upon these people or the institution and the reciprocal effect upon him may be concentrated upon. Conceptualizing the discussion at this stage may offer the client or patient a sufficiently discerning glimpse of the next higher truth to stimulate his movement in that direction. Abroms also makes the point that the therapist might recognize that an individual at a fairly high stage level may be living a life that neglects some of the requirements for fulfillment at a lower level. Thus, a principled client may not be enjoying his proper due at the level of sensuality characteristic of stage 2. Upon making such a diagnosis, the therapist should assist the client in experiencing that aspect of stage 2 which he has an ethical right to.

Abroms's contribution consists of adapting Kohlberg's stage theory to the psychotherapeutic enterprise in a manner that lends much greater precision to assessment and differential intervention than has prevailed in many quarters. Although the overall goal is value change achieved by stimulating developmental progression, he has also achieved greater precision in goal setting by specifying subgoals corresponding to each stage in the hierarchy. Abroms has redefined the therapist's technical competence and has set an unconventional goal for the therapeutic process. His formulation is a reconceptualization that is both creative and innovative. He maintains that the position he espouses joins both humanism and science, further asserting that as the helper leads the helpee toward the construction of higher spiritual values he is by definition helping him to achieve a more adaptive knowledge of reality.

### Promoting Role Taking Competence

Chandler, in "Egocentrism and Antisocial Behavior," has reported good results in combining drama and filming techniques, subjects rotating at playing character roles, and subsequent group discussions in work with delinquent boys. Role-taking competence increased in the participants and their rate of recidivism significantly reduced in comparison to control and placebo groups. Staub found ("The Use of Role Playing and Induction), that training in role-taking skills led to a differential effect in the prosocial behavior of boys and girls. Boys subsequently exhibited increased sharing behavior and girls increased helping behavior. Chandler, Greenspan, and Barenboim conducted an experiment, described in "Assessment and Training of Role-Taking and Referential Communication Skills," with emotionally disturbed institutionalized children who were divided into three groups. There were two experimental groups, one of which received role-taking training, a second of which received referential communication training. Referential communication refers to the speaker's ability to select the most appropriate word in his vocabulary to convey his meaning while taking into account both the context within which he is speaking and the informational needs of the listener. A third group received no training. The two training groups demonstrated significant postintervention improvement compared to the control group. The role-taking group utilized video filming techniques in which the children rotated opportunities to portray disparate characters, thereby giving them practice at taking the perspectives of others. In the referential communication group, children were given feedback when they delivered inadequate messages. It was predicted that the feedback would create cognitive conflict and out of the dissonance they would reconstruct the messages more accurately. It is of interest that those children who received referential training only improved both in that area and in role-taking. The children who trained in role-taking improved in that area, but showed no improvement in referential communication. It is likely that referential communication demands role-taking competence as a precondition, hence while training at the former, the latter is also developed. Role-taking competence, however, does not automatically imply referential communication skills.

The most extensive and highly conceptualized efforts directed at applying sociomoral knowledge in a cognitive-developmental framework to clinical practice have been emanating from the Judge Baker Guidance Center in Boston, frequently in collaboration with Harvard University. The leader in this pioneering undertaking, which has been gaining recognition over the last several years, has been Robert Selman, the director of the Guidance Center. Selman's conceptual orientation to role-taking and its relationship to moral development have been presented in chapter 3. Paralleling these structural developments are qualitiatively increasingly more complex stages of interpersonal conceptions which children acquire with age. The various components of development as seen in Piaget's, Kohlberg's, and Selman's work are all interrelated as structural wholes. Selman's work is geared to making a diagnosis of how this all comes to bear upon a child's competence at social reasoning. Developmental lags which may be instrumental in causing or maintaining emotional disturbance are diagnosed, and attempts are then made to stimulate development with a view toward improving social functioning. Strategies of intervention are designed with the specific aim of furthering development in role-taking and interpersonal conceptions. Selman is clear in conveying that he does not see a cognitive-structural approach as replacing more traditional psychodynamic models, but as an alternate orientation that may offer a greater clinical yield in some cases, depending upon the problem.

In one clinical vignette, recounted in "Social Cognitive Understanding," Selman describes diagnosis and intervention with a ten-year-old boy who was at an egocentric level generally found in children at ages four and five. Upon observation it was discovered that when he interacted with others he appeared not to be making any differentiation between what he was feeling and what others might be feeling. He failed to evidence any role-taking capacities and, hence, his interpersonal relationships were shorn of reciprocity. He expected that his needs would be gratified immediately and, of course, failed to take into account what other people's perspective of that expectation might be. In fact, since he could not role-take, he had no way of knowing that from another person's point of view his needs may often remain unknown unless explicitly communicated by him. Selman's young client, like many an adult, would feel that he was hated when his uncommunicated needs were not being met. In fact, the young boy was disliked, but this was the result of the deficiency in his social reasoning, rather than any inherent inclination on the part of others to turn against him. The intervention strategy was to give him a concentrated experience over a period of time in a therapeutic camp at differentiating between his own and other people's feelings and thoughts. He was helped to seek out internal causes of behavior in other people and to take their point of view. He was constantly informed about the usual expectations that other people would have of him in different situations. At the end of eight weeks his conception of friendship had matured, he had shifted from being completely egocentric to evidencing some role-taking ability, and his popularity had increased to the point where he had acquired many friends. The strategy adopted in this case can be adapted to a variety of settings. When the child is not as accessible around the clock, the way this child was in a summer camp or another may be in a residential treatment center, the parents may be trained by the helper to continue the intervention at home. A secondary benefit of doing this is enlisting the parents in a constructive activity which may promote in them a sense of being directly helpful to their child. The increase in positive interaction between parent and child may itself be beneficial. Furthermore, conceptualization of the problem in this manner avoids the dilemma of pointing an accusatory finger at the parents, who so often feel either guilty or defensive about their child's problem. Lastly, this orientation does not label the child as sick, but views him as in need of developmental stimulation to further development in social reasoning along its normal course.

Selman, in citing another example, demonstrated how a refined diagnosis from a sociocognitive perspective can provide valuable supplementary material to other data-obtaining methods. A fourteen-year-old adolescent was brought to the clinic by his mother because he was socially isolated and had not been promoted to the next grade the previous year due to a school phobia. He seemed to have low self-esteem and was fearful of entering into social relations. The clinic team decided to administer the Heinz dilemma from Kohlberg's repertoire of moral dilemmas. Asked whether Heinz should steal the drug to save his wife's life, he replied that he should do so only if he loves her. If he does not love her, then there is no point in risking jail. The boy elaborated further that Heinz should steal for her only if he needs her. Asked if Heinz should steal the drug to save himself, the adolescent replied that Heinz should not, explaining that he, the boy, would not steal the drug to save himself because he was not worth it. Asked to explain further, he pointed out that he does not have a lot of money and, therefore, is not important. In discussing capital punishment he came out in favor of it because he would not want to spend a lifetime in prison. Encouraged to see it from the point of view of other hypothetical prisoners he could not entertain the possibility that any of them would have a different perspective. He sensed that they would have a perspective, but he failed to differentiate it from his own. In Selman's analysis the youngster is seen as being at stages 1 and 2 in both role-taking and moral development, even though by his age most young people would be at stage 3 in both areas, some as high as stage 4 in role-taking. His view of saving the wife's life reflected an instrumental orientation, stage 2, in moral development since it was based on his own need gratification and had nothing to do with respect for her as a person. His orientation regarding the preservation of his own life was at stage 1, being based upon a purely materialistic conception of his own worth. This cognitive structural aspect of his development clearly coincides with his feelings of low self-esteem. Selman conveys, ". . . not that cognition is cause and feelings are effect, but that cognition and feelings about the self and about others are inseparable."[8] Despite the lag in the moral area he was functioning at a low formal operational level in his performance on Piaget's and Inhelder's cognitive tasks in the physics area, reflecting good scientific reasoning for his age. However, he scored at the concrete operational level in his social reasoning. Selman suggests that his lack of social interaction offered him little opportunity to test out his interpersonal and social hypotheses, in the fashion that adolescents would normally do, often with great vigor. The point of such an analysis is to individualize the client, understand him from his own phenomenological perspective, and to assess from this information the strategic entry level for developmental intervention. In a general statement encompassing his basic orientation, Selman expresses the following:

> Determining the stage of cognitive or social development of a particular child leads the professional to understand how the child looks at the world, and to avoid expectations of conceptual and emotional abilities that the child has not yet developed. Far from disdaining the value of understanding the child's interpersonal dynamics, this approach enhances that understanding by exploring the stage and by identifying the next stage toward which his development can be directed.[9]

## THE ORGANIZATIONAL PERSPECTIVE

To illustrate an imaginative and novel application of Kohlberg's orientation in an often neglected milieu with underserved populations, let us turn to intervention within the correctional field. Kohlberg, Scharf, and Hickey conducted a series of pilot studies which ended in 1972, described in "The Justice Structure of the Prison." Since that time they have elaborated at some length upon the theory and rationale utilized in those pioneering efforts in "The Just Community Approach to Corrections." The goal of the studies was to implement moral development programs among inmates and staff of correctional institutions as a form of rehabilitation. The approach was one of "justice as treatment" in contrast to previous inefficacious attempts at rehabilitation. Work with offenders in early society had emphasized retribution and moral reform. Imprisonment and punishment were ways of extracting the price one had to pay for the offense. There existed a climate of moralism in which prisoners were subject to persuasion and sermonizing with the expectation that they would add such traits as honesty, restraint, and respect for authority to their "bag of virtues," as Kohlberg is fond of saying. These methods proved unsuccessful. The traditional approach of attempting to produce reform by altering moral character gave way to a modern viewpoint, adopted by many professionals, that offenders are sick and should receive psychotherapy. Programs directed at psychotherapy have not demonstrated any greater success than the historical emphasis upon reform by modifying moral character. An alternate modern approach has been the use of behavior therapy technology. Although some immediate gains in modifying behavior have been observed through the use of token systems which dispense rewards for desired behaviors, long-range benefits have been minimal. This was predictable as the emotions, cognitions, and values of the prisoners were ignored. Since it is difficult, if not impossible, to maintain the reward system in the natural environment upon release, newly acquired behaviors were eventually extinguished. It is true that psychotherapy does deal with feelings and attitudes, but there is little focus upon the existential reality the prisoner encounters daily in relationships with security officers and fellow prisoners. A vacuum existed in terms of effective rehabilitation programs, which Kohlberg and his collaborators have been trying to fill.

In what has come to be known as the Cheshire Experiment, Kohlberg and his collaborators investigated the justice structure of a reformatory located in Cheshire, Connecticut. In addition, they collected data on the moral stages of prisoners. The prisoners' judgments on moral dilemmas, designed to test their perceptions of justice both outside and inside of the prison, were sought. In examining the justice structure of the institution, it was clear that prisoners were completely subjected to the authority of the administration. They held no decision-making power whatsoever. Rewards and punishments were not uncommonly dispensed arbitrarily by staff. There existed no avenue for appealing abuses. Punishments were sometimes disproportionately harsh for minor infractions of rules and sometimes administered by a guard as a means to vent a personal dislike toward a prisoner. The discipline board that prevailed did not feel obligated to offer rational explanations for punishment meted out. Certain privi-

leges were accorded to influential prisoners by staff to elicit cooperation in exchange. From this analysis it was concluded that the justice
structure operated at stage 4 insofar as there did exist definite bureaucratic rules which inmates were expected to conform to, with no
opportunity to have the rules reconsidered, much less modified. It
was also found to be operating at stage 2 insofar as staff indulged
their own needs and bestowed rewards in anticipation of a reciprocal
exchange that would benefit them. It is against this description of the
prisoners' reality that their moral perceptions can most fruitfully be
considered. The inmates tended to perceive the prison as functioning
at a premoral level, encompassing both stages 1 and 2. Their relationships with other prisoners they mostly viewed as being at stage 2,
hence predicated upon instrumental exchanges. The justice of the
prison administration was identified by inmates as coercively demanding obedience and, therefore, assigned to stage 1 by most of
them. Perceptions by inmates of how the prison was actually run
proved to be independent of their scores on normative moral judgments. A comparison was made between inmates' proposed resolutions to hypothetical moral dilemmas involving the prison environment and the nonprison dilemmas of the standard variety. There
appeared to be a significant difference in moral judgments, depending upon whether the inside or outside environment was being
evaluated. In general, the moral reasoning was at a lower level when
considering dilemmas within the prison context, as compared to
judgments about moral dilemmas based upon stories that were not
prison-related. Not a single inmate demonstrated a higher level on a
prison-related dilemma in comparison to a nonprison dilemma. Inmates who exhibited as high as stage 3 and even stage 4 on standard
moral dilemmas were scored at stage 1 and 2 when responding to
prison-related dilemmas. Thus it is seen that the impact of the environment has a decided influence upon the moral judgment of the individual. This finding was typical not only at Cheshire, but at other
prisons as well. It is important, however, not to overestimate the level
of moral development attained by most offenders independently of
the prison environment. Kohlberg, Kaufman, Scharf, and Hickey report:

> A variety of studies in the United States and other countries indicate that
> criminal offenders are remarkably lower in moral judgment development
> than are non-offenders of the same social background. In fact, the ma-

STRATEGIES FOR INTERVENTION *175*

jority (75 per cent) of non-criminal adolescents and young adults are at Stage 3 or 4, while the majority of adolescent offenders are at Stage 1 or 2.[10]

This information is vital in appreciating the rationale of the moral development programs designed by Kohlberg.

The Cheshire intervention was comprised primarily of moral discussion groups which resulted in small gains for some in moral maturity. A two-year follow-up did show that those who had advanced were less subject to recidivism than released prisoners who had not participated. However, the overall moral atmosphere of the prison justice structure placed severe restraints on what could be achieved. Furthermore, life within the prison provided no role-taking opportunities such as might be stimulated by the availability of leadership roles, flexible dialogue with open-ended outcomes, and decision-making powers. The Cheshire experience led to the design of a more comprehensive treatment model, which was mounted in 1971 at the Niantic State Farm for Women. By the time the experiment had been functioning for two years, only 16 percent of those women who had been discharged either returned or once again had encountered some kind of trouble with the authorities. Many of the women had even gone on to create quite stabilized and decent lives. This was not the case for all, however. (In 1973 the experiment was enlarged to continue with "justice as treatment" in a community-based facility, where some of the inmates were permitted to finish their sentences.) The difference introduced at Niantic was that the experiment became a total experience. The institution had agreed to reshape its policies so that the participants were permitted to assume self-governing responsibilities. Nine staff were trained by the Kohlberg team, which served as trainers and consultants. Staff assumed the role of discussion leaders and facilitators. They had to be trained, for example, to avoid falling into the trap of becoming preoccupied with the content and outcome of management issues, as opposed to their proper role of facilitating discussion among inmates, with a focus on moral issues. It would be up to the inmates as a cohesive self-governing group to determine policies of right and wrong behavior and to recommend *just* disciplinary action for violations.

In the early training sessions with line staff, they voiced many of their own complaints, but following sufficient time for ventilation, they shifted to a problem-solving orientation. Put simply by Kohlberg et al., "The involved staff members committed themselves to an intervention which, working from a moral development framework, would address the problems of the institution."[11] It became apparent that their function was not viewed as being exclusively custodial; but although they had wanted to be helpful to the inmates, they lacked leadership and a theoretically grounded practice model to work with. The inmates' early sessions focused on very specific recommendations which were personal and idiosyncratic and, hence, did not offer a basis for forging out a policy document to govern their behavior. As the level of discussions became transformed, there emerged a working constitution that was accepted as law by all members of the experimental community. As might have been anticipated, a preliminary problem that demanded attention was the mutual distrust that occurred between staff and inmates. The Kohlberg team served as mediators and eventually this obstacle, undoubtedly an inevitable one, was surmounted. One of the major objectives of the training model was to create a moral climate for the inmates which was at least at their own level or higher. Community meetings, almost always called by inmates, could be invoked by staff or inmates to resolve issues of discipline as they would arise. Each person had only one vote, including staff. The Kohlberg team has made the point that for many of the women in this project the constitution, which they had participated in establishing, was the first objectified set of rules and regulations they had had a genuine stake in. This is essentially different from traditional small-group treatment. Participants are more involved in the total matrix of operations. Emphasis is upon promoting their moral development to stage 3, where they will experience some group loyalty and concern about others' feelings toward them, which clearly goes beyond the hedonistic-instrumentalist orientation of stage 2. There is an even more ambitious goal, albeit a realistic one, of stimulating moral development to stage 4, where the inmate at that stage would become a citizen of the community with a commitment to uphold the laws which she has had a part in creating. In addition to special community meetings to deal with emergent problems, regular small group meetings are held. Fears and dilemmas that are very real to the women, some prison-based and others related to the outside, provide the grist for the discussion mill. The discussions are led in such a way as to facilitate and heighten role-taking capabilities. Alternate perspectives to what others are saying are deliberately elicited. Logical analysis of problems is invited. Conflicts inherent in competing claims are brought into prominence and higher stage exposure emerges in discussion, as not all of the discussants are at the same level. It is the role of the leader to sharpen the nature of the conflict and to take some responsibility for introducing higher stage reasoning. Indoctrination and didactic teaching are avoided at all times. Structural mode of reasoning and developmental progress are stressed over content and sermonizing. As has been seen throughout this book, structural advance is not an isolated psychic phenomenon. Moral stages reflect distinctly the organization of social and interpersonal knowledge in an individual. They generate rules and ultimately principles that play a strong governing role in behavior.

The actual creation of a just community is the essence of the treatment provided by the moral development program model. Kohlberg et al. capture this well in formulating the following:

> We can see that democracy is central to moral development if we see that the heart of morality is a sense of fairness and justice. Morality means a decision of what is right where there is a conflict between the interests and claims of two or more people. Justice means fairness in deciding the conflict, giving each person his due and being impartial to all. . . . While most inmates do not care about society's morality, they do care about justice or fairness. Because they feel they are treated unjustly and live in an unjust world they do not try to be fair to others. To be motivated to act fairly, inmates must feel they are part of a just community.[12]

As a follow-up to the preceding comments, Kohlberg et al. continue:

> In interviews with inmates two years after release, many who were functioning well outside expressed why they thought the programme had led to significant changes in their lives. They said that for the first time they had lived in a setting where people treated each other fairly and with mutual concern. On leaving the programme they had decided that they wanted to have lives in which they could continue to have such relationships and choose life patterns which could enable them to do that.[13]

## CONCLUSION

The interventive methods that have been under discussion in this chapter are firmly anchored in the cognitive-developmental sociomoral tradition of Piaget and Kohlberg. They certainly do not exclude other approaches and, indeed, have not as yet attained a high level of technical refinement. Each method, either explicitly or implicitly, employs tactics designed to promote greater objective relativism by facilitating the subject's decentering process in the sociocognitive moral realm. In each approach a dimunition of embeddedness in the egocentrism of one's present perspective is sought in favor of development toward a greater capacity for identifying, coordinating, and synthesizing multiple perspectives. Success in such an endeavor is virtually seen as the construction of a higher and more adaptive level of sociomoral knowledge. In all cases the interventionist has a clear idea of the direction he believes it is necessary for the subject to move toward if more adaptive behavior is to be achieved. The interventionist adopts a directive-catalytic role rather than a passive-neutral stance in the change procedure. The method in each approach is not interpretive, but instead entails the disclosure of the subject's phenomenological state, followed by a strategy for facilitating the transformation of that state into the perspective characteristic of the next stage in the universal developmental sequence. Adopting a developmental framework deemphasizes pathology and the overworked medical model in favor of an outlook emphasizing positive change and growth. It also reduces the dichotomous structure of the therapeutic situation as consisting of one sick person and one well person, replacing it with a view of two or more participants, all of whom share in a potentially ongoing process as developing persons.

Despite the shared commitment to a cognitive-developmental framework and the commonalities described above, there are differences among the interventionists examined here that are worth identifying. Selman and Chandler have been very specific in citing concrete techniques that lend themselves to direct application. These techniques are designed primarily to foster role-taking competence in subjects whose interpersonal relationships appear dysfunctional due to a limited capacity to see the other's point of view. In the strategies of Abroms, Kegan, and Kohlberg we find their interventive methods formulated in broader terms.[14]

Abroms is distinct from all of the others in that he is a psychiatrist whose professional education was not based upon a cognitive-developmental perspective, which he has embraced only recently. Therefore, it is not surprising that he has attempted to link more conventional treatment approaches to corresponding stages in the cognitive-developmental sequences. In other words, for example, biological, behavioral, and family treatment approaches form a hierarchy of their own which may conceivably be most appropriately implemented in relation to the stage development of the subject or patient in question. It is also my impression that Abroms is perhaps the most openly avid advocate of psychotherapy as a value change procedure.

The work of Kegan is the most theoretically ambitious, as he struggles vigorously to develop a psychodynamic model that goes beyond the basic Piaget-Kohlberg paradigm. His work is demanding and requires that one grapple with his ideas through repeated encounters with them. Even by the most liberal literary standards, some of Kegan's passages fail to yield a clear and unequivocal meaning. Nevertheless, the total impact of his formulations suggests to me a stunning breakthrough to a new reconceptualization of personality theory and development. Although all cognitive-developmental theory has a strong phenomenological component, it is in the work of Kegan that each individual's way of knowing-in-the-world is brought to its sharpest focus. This is accomplished largely by integrating existential and developmental themes into a single model. Although Kegan has formulated an enlightened view of the helping process, and this is especially true of his comments regarding the relationship between the helper and helpee, he has not as yet presented specific techniques to guide the helper in his efforts to promote development.

It is in their attempts to create "just communities" within prison and school environments that Kohlberg and his colleagues have exhibited the broadest spatio-temporal approach to intervention. Integral to any attempt at altering the sociocognitive moral structure of the individual is an equally concentrated effort at modifying the environmental structure. The way to promote individual moral development is to create a total community that fosters conditions conducive to it. A repressive and excessively authoritative climate is inimical to moral growth. An organizational context, on the other hand, which provides direct participation in democratic decision-making and role-taking opportunities related to the everyday lives of the individuals involved will maximize the potential for moral growth. In adopting this position, Kohlberg's Piagetian roots are highlighted, as we recall Piaget's emphasis upon the growing child's evolution toward genuine cooperation and reciprocity.

As further progress is made in developing change methodologies for this field, we might look forward to an increased range of interventive applications and an accompanying advance in the identification of more specific strategies and tactics. We might also reasonably anticipate attempts at integration with other models of helping and practice techniques, as well as the use of these approaches in the exercise of responsible eclecticism.

# Notes

## 1. A Cognitive-Structural Foundation

1. Kohlberg, "Early Education," p. 104.
2. Flavell, *Cognitive Development,* p. 105.

## 2. Piagetian Roots in Moral Judgment

1. Piaget, *Moral Judgment of the Child,* pp. 42–43.
2. *Ibid.,* p. 65.
3. *Ibid.,* p. 111.
4. *Ibid.,* p. 138.
5. *Ibid.,* p. 174.
6. Kohlberg, "Development of Moral Character and Moral Ideology," pp. 397–98.
7. Piaget, *Moral Judgment of the Child,* p. 295.
8. *Ibid.,* p. 394.
9. Kohlberg, *Moral Character,* pp. 397–98.
10. Lickona, "Research on Piaget's Theory of Moral Development," p. 240.
11. *Ibid.,* p. 235.

## 3. Egocentrism and Social Perspectivism

1. Inhelder and Piaget, *The Growth of Logical Thinking from Childhood to Adolescence,* p. 345.
2. Kohlberg, "Moral Stages and Moralization: The Cognitive-Developmental Approach," p. 49.
3. Kohlberg, "Stage and Sequence," p. 398.
4. *Ibid.,* p. 402.

5. Deutsch and Kraus, *Theories in Social Psychology*.

6. Gruber and Vonèche, *The Essential Piaget*, p. 92.

7. Elkind, "Egocentrism in Children and Adolescents," p. 91.

8. Feffer, "The Cognitive Implications of Role-Taking Behavior"; Feffer and Gourevitch, "Cognitive Aspects of Role-Taking in Children"; Feffer and Suchotliff, "Decentering Implications of Social Interactions"; Feffer, "Developmental Analysis of Interpersonal Behavior."

9. Feffer, "Developmental Analysis of Interpersonal Behavior," p. 211.

10. Flavell et al., *The Development of Role-Taking and Communication Skills in Children*, p. 5.

11. Miller, Kessel, and Falvell, "Thinking About Thinking About People," p. 622.

12. Selman, "The Relation of Social Perspective-Taking to Moral Development"; Selman and Damon, "The Necessity (but insufficiency) of Social Perspective Taking for Conceptions of Justice at Three Early Levels"; Selman, "Social Cognitive Understanding."

13. Robert L. Selman, "Toward a Structural Analysis of Developing Interpersonal Relations Concepts."

14. The figures reported by Selman in the text of his paper do not coincide with those appearing in table 8, p. 33 of the paper. I have cited the figures in the table, which leaves one case unaccounted for.

15. Kurdek, "Perspective Taking As the Cognitive Basis of Children's Moral Development," pp. 22–23.

## 4. THE STAGE THEORY OF MORAL DEVELOPMENT

1. Kohlberg, "The Development of Children's Orientation Toward a Moral Order," p. 30.

2. Kohlberg, "Moral Stages and Moralization," p. 36.

3. Kohlberg, "Moral Judgment Interview and Procedures for Scoring."

4. Kohlberg, "From Is to Ought," p. 199.

5. Kohlberg and Turiel, "Moral Development and Education," p. 416.

6. Kohlberg, "From Is to Ought," pp. 202, 204.

7. Kohlberg and Elfenbein, "Moral Judgments Concerning Capital Punishment."

8. Quoted in Muss, "Kohlberg's Cognitive-Developmental Approach," p. 46.

9. Kohlberg, "Stages of Moral Development"; "From Is to Ought"; "The Claim to Moral Adequacy."

10. The Heinz story is ideally constructed to serve Kohlberg's purpose. Should the reader think, however, that Heinz's dilemma is remote from real life, it is worth noting that at the time of this writing (1978), the State of Pennsylvania, due to a bureaucratic impasse, has temporarily discontinued reimbursing druggists for services to welfare recipients. The result is that many druggists have stopped filling the prescriptions for these people and,

therefore, thousands of poor people have at present gone for weeks without needed medicine.

11. Kohlberg, "Stages of Moral Development," p. 61.
12. Kohlberg "The Development of Moral Judgments," p. 633.
13. Kohlberg, "The Claim to Moral Adequacy," p. 641.
14. Kohlberg and Elfenbein, "Capital Punishment," p. 637.
15. *Ibid.*
16. Kohlberg and Kramer, "Adult Moral Development," and Kohlberg, "Adult Moral Development Revisited."
17. "Adult Moral Development," p. 114.
18. *Ibid.*, p. 115.
19. Kohlberg, "Adult Moral Development Revisited," p. 21.
20. Turiel, "Stage Transition in Moral Development," p. 750.
21. Kohlberg, "Adult Moral Development Revisited," pp. 30–31.

## 5. ACTION, HIERARCHY, AND LOGIC

1. Krebs and Kohlberg, "Moral Judgment and Ego Controls as Determinants of Resistance to Cheating," p. 33.
2. *Ibid.*, p. 32.
3. Kohlberg, "From Is to Ought," p. 229.
4. Haan, Smith, and Block, "Moral Reasoning of Young Adults," p. 197.
5. Haan, "Hypothetical and Actual Moral Reasoning," p. 268.
6. Turiel, "Stage Transition in Moral Development," p. 737.
7. Kohlberg, "Education for Justice," p. 82.
8. Turiel, "Developmental Processes in the Child's Moral Thinking," p. 127.
9. *Ibid.*, pp. 129–30.
10. Kohlberg, "Education for Justice," p. 58.
11. Dewey, *The Quest for Certainty*, p. 255.
12. Dewey, *Reconstruction in Philosophy*, pp. 163–64.
13. Kohlberg, "The Concepts of Developmental Psychology as the Central Guide to Education," p. 14.
14. Kuhn et al., "The Development of Formal Operations in Logical and Moral Judgment," p. 170.
15. *Ibid.*, p. 178.
16. *Ibid.*, p. 141.
17. *Ibid.*, p. 142.

## 6. METHODOLOGICAL AND THEORETICAL CRITIQUE

1. Peters, "Moral Development," p. 258.
2. *Ibid.*, p. 259.
3. Alston, "Comments on Kohlberg's 'From Is to Ought,' " pp. 276–77.
4. Simpson, "Moral Development Research," pp. 85–86.

5. *Ibid.,* p. 94.

6. *Ibid.,* p. 95.

7. Although it does not stress cross-cultural scoring, a scoring manual is available through the Harvard Center for Moral Education. It is revised periodically, the most recent revision having occurred the summer of 1978.

8. Kuhn, "Short-Term Longitudinal Evidence for the Sequentiality of Kohlberg's Early Stages of Moral Judgment," p. 166.

9. Gibbs, "Kohlberg's Stages of Moral Judgment," pp. 55–56.

10. *Ibid.,* p. 57.

11. Hall and Davis, *Moral Education in Theory and Practice,* p. 104.

12. Simpson, "Moral Development Research," p. 97.

13. *Ibid.,* p. 98.

14. Puka, "Moral Education and Its Cure," p. 57.

15. Gilligan, "In a Different Voice," p. 484.

16. *Ibid.,* p. 491.

17. *Ibid.,* p. 514.

18. *Ibid.,* p. 515.

## 7. CONCEPTS AND STRATEGIES FOR INTERVENTION

1. Kegan, "Ego and Truth," pp. 344–45.

2. The reader is cautioned against attaching a connotation of altruism to this term.

3. Kegan, "Ego and Truth," p. 190.

4. *Ibid.,* pp. 191–92.

5. *Ibid.,* p. 323.

6. Abroms, "The Place of Values in Psychotherapy," p. 12.

7. *Ibid.,* p. 14.

8. Selman, "Social Cognitive Understanding," p. 315.

9. *Ibid.,* p. 300.

10. Kohlberg et al., "The Just Community Approach to Corrections," p. 256.

11. Kohlberg, Scharf, and Hickey, "The Justice Structure of the Prison," p. 9.

12. Kohlberg et al., "The Just Community Approach to Corrections," pp. 247–48.

13. *Ibid.,* p. 248.

14. Selman's theoretical contribution, of course, includes broadly conceptualized developmental stages of social perspective taking.

# Bibliography

Abroms, Gene. "The Place of Values in Psychotherapy." *Journal of Marriage and Family Counseling* (October 1978), 4:3–17.

Alston, William P. "Comments on Kohlberg's 'From Is to Ought.' " In T. Mischel, ed., *Cognitive Development and Epistemology*, pp. 269–84. New York: Academic Press, 1971.

Berrigan, Philip and John Schuchardt. Letters to the Editor. *The Philadelphia Inquirer*. Philadelphia, Pa., appx. 1978.

Broughton, John. "The Cognitive-Developmental Approach to Morality." *Journal of Moral Education* (January 1978), 7:81–96.

Brown, Michael E., S. H. Schwartz, K. A. Feldman, and A. Heingarter. "Some Personality Correlates of Conduct in Two Situations of Moral Conflict." *Journal of Personality* (1969), 37:41–57.

Brown, Roger and Richard J. Herrnstein. *Psychology*. Boston: Little, Brown, 1975.

Burton, Roger V. "Honesty and Dishonesty." In Thomas Lickona, ed., *Moral Development and Behavior: Theory, Research, and Social Issues*, pp. 173–97. New York: Holt, Rinehart & Winston, 1976.

Byrne, Diane. "Role-Taking in Adolescence." Doctoral dissertation, Harvard University, 1973.

Chandler, Michael. "Egocentrism and Antisocial Behavior: The Assessment and Training of Social Perspective-Taking Skills." *Developmental Psychology* (1973), 9:326–32.

—— "Social Cognition." In *Knowledge and Development*, pp. 93–147. Edited by Willis F. Overton and Jeanette McCarthy Gallagher. New York: Plenum Press, 1977.

Chandler, Michael, Stephen Greenspan, and Carl Barenboim. "Assessment and Training of Role-Taking and Referential Communication Skills in Institutionalized Emotionally Disturbed Children." *Developmental Psychology* (1974), 10:546–53.

Deutsch, Morton and Robert M. Kraus. *Theories in Social Psychology*. New York: Basic Books, 1965.

Dewey, John. *The Quest for Certainty*. New York: Minton, Balch, and Company, 1930.

—— *Reconstruction in Philosophy*. New York: Mentor Books, 1950.

Elkind, David. "Egocentrism in Children and Adolescents." *Children and Adolescents: Interpretive Essays on Jean Piaget*, pp. 74–95. 2d ed. New York: Oxford University Press, 1974.

Feffer, Melvin. "The Cognitive Implications of Role-Taking Behavior." *Journal of Personality* (1959), 27:152–68.

—— "Developmental Analysis of Interpersonal Behavior." *Psychological Review* (1970), 77:197–214.

Feffer, Melvin and Vivian Gourevitch. "Cognitive Aspects of Role-Taking in Children." *Journal of Personality* (1960), 28:384–96.

Feffer, Melvin and Leonard Suchotliff. "Decentering Implications of Social Interactions." *Personality and Social Psychology* (1966), 4:415–22.

Flavell, John H. *The Developmental Psychology of Jean Piaget*. New York: Van Nostrand, 1963.

—— *Cognitive Development*. Englewood Cliffs, N.J.: Prentice-Hall, 1977.

Flavell, John H., P. T. Botkin, C. L. Fry, J. W. Wright, and P. E. Jarvis. *The Development of Role-Taking and Communication Skills in Children*. New York: Wiley, 1968.

Gardner, Howard. *The Quest for Mind*. New York: Knopf, 1973.

Gibbs, John C. "'Kohlberg's Stages of Moral Judgment: A Constructive Critique." *Harvard Educational Review* (1977), 47:43–59.

Gilligan, Carol. "In a Different Voice: Women's Conceptions of Self and Morality." *Harvard Educational Review* (1977), 47:481–517.

Gruber, Howard and Jacques J. Vonèche, eds. *The Essential Piaget*. New York: Basic Books, 1977.

Gutkin, Daniel C. "An Analysis of the Concept of Moral Intentionality." *Human Development* (1973), 16:371–81.

Haan, Norma. "Activism As a Moral Protest: Moral Judgments of Hypothetical Dilemmas and an Actual Situation of Civil Disobedience." Cambridge: Harvard University, 1973. Mimeo.

—— "Hypothetical and Actual Moral Reasoning in a Situation of Civil Disobedience." *Journal of Personality and Social Psychology* (1975), 32:255–70.

Haan, Norma, Brewster Smith, and Jeanne Block. "Moral Reasoning of Young Adults: Political Social Behavior, Family Background, and Personality Correlates." *Journal of Personality and Social Psychology* (1968), 10:183–201.

Hall, Robert T. and John V. Davis. *Moral Education in Theory and Practice*. Buffalo, N.Y.: Prometheus, 1975.

Hartshorne, H. and M. A. May. *Studies in the Nature of Character:* Vol. 1, *Studies in Deceit*, 1928; Vol. 2, *Studies in Service and Self-Control*, 1929; Vol. 3, *Studies in the Organization of Character*, 1930 (with F. K. Shuttleworth). New York: Macmillan, 1928–1930.

Hoffman, Martin L. "Moral Development," In P. Mussen, ed., *Carmichael's Manual of Child Psychology*, 1:261–359. New York: Wiley, 1970.

Holstein, C. "Development of Moral Judgment: A Longitudinal Study of Males and Females." *Child Development* (1976), 47:51–61.

Inhelder, Bärbel and Jean Piaget. *The Growth of Logical Thinking from Childhood to Adolescence*. Translated by A. Parsons and S. Milgram. New York: Basic Books, 1958. Originally published, 1955.

Inhelder, Bärbel, Hermine Sinclair, and Magali Bovet. *Learning and the Development of Cognition*. Translated by S. Wedgwood. Cambridge: Harvard University Press, 1974.

Keasey, Charles. "Implications of Cognitive Development for Moral Reasoning." In D. J. DePalma and J. M. Foley, eds., *Moral Development: Current Theory and Research*, pp. 39–56. New York: Lawrence Erlbaum, 1975.

Keats, J. A., K. F. Collis, and G. S. Halford, eds. *Cognitive Development: Research Based on a Neo-Piagetian Approach*. New York: Wiley, 1978.

Kegan, Robert. "Ego and Truth: Personality and the Piaget Paradigm." Doctoral dissertation, Harvard University, 1977.

Kohlberg, Lawrence. "The Development of Modes of Moral Thinking and Choice in the Years Ten to Sixteen." Doctoral dissertation, University of Chicago, 1958.

—— "The Development of Children's Orientation Toward a Moral Order 1. Sequence in the Development of Moral Thought." *Vita Humana* (1963), 6:11–33.

—— "Development of Moral Character and Moral Ideology." L. W. Hoffman, ed., *Review of Child Development Research*, 1:383–431. New York: Russell Sage Foundation, 1964.

—— "Stage and Sequence: The Cognitive-Developmental Approach to Socialization." In G. Goslin, ed., *Handbook of Socialization*, pp. 347–480. Chicago: Rand McNally, 1969.

—— "Education for Justice: A Modern Statement of the Platonic View." In T. Sizen, ed., *Moral Education*, pp. 57–84. Cambridge: Harvard University Press, 1970.

Kohlberg, Lawrence. "Stages of Moral Development As a Basis for Moral Education." In C. M. Beck, B. S. Crittender, and E. V. Sullivan, eds., *Moral Education*, pp. 24–92. New York: Neuman Press, 1971.

—— "From Is to Ought: How to Commit the Naturalistic Fallacy and Get Away with It in the Study of Moral Development." In Theodore Mischel, ed., *Cognitive Development and Epistemology*, pp. 151–235. New York: Academic Press, 1971.

—— "Early Education: A Cognitive Developmental View." In P. S. Sears, ed., *Intellectual Development*, pp. 100–42. New York: Wiley, 1971.

—— "Indoctrination Versus Relativity." Paper presented at Harvard University at the eighteenth summer conference of the Institute on Religion in an Age of Science, Star Island, New Hampshire, July 31–August 6, 1971.

—— "Continuities in Childhood and Adult Moral Development Revisited," in *Collected Papers on Moral Development and Moral Education*. Cambridge: Center for Moral Education, Harvard University, 1973.

—— "The Claim to Moral Adequacy of a Highest Stage of Moral Judgment." The *Journal of Philosophy* (1937), 70:630–46.

—— "Stages and Aging in Moral Development: Some Speculations." *Gerontologist* (1973), 13:497–502.

—— "Education, Moral Development and Faith." *Journal of Moral Education* (1974), 4:5–16.

—— "The Cognitive-Developmental Approach: New Developments and a Response to Criticisms." Paper presented in the Symposium on Moral Development and Behavior, biannual convention of the Society for Research in Child Development, Denver, April 1975.

—— "Moral Stages and Moralization: The Cognitive-Developmental Approach." In Thomas Lickona, ed., *Moral Development and Behavior: Theory, Research, and Social Issues*, pp. 31–53. New York: Holt, Rinehart, & Winston, 1976.

—— "Moral Judgment Interview and Procedures for Scoring." Cambridge: Center for Moral Education, Harvard University, 1976. Mimeo.

—— "The Concepts of Developmental Psychology As the Central Guide to Education: Examples from Cognitive, Moral, and Psychological Education." In M. C. Reynolds, ed., *Proceedings of the Conference on Psychology and the Process of Schooling in the Next Decade: Alternative Conceptions*. Leadership Training Institute, sponsored by Bureau for Educational Personnel Department, U.S. Office of Education, date unknown.

Kohlberg, Lawrence, ed. *Recent Research in Moral Development.* New York: Holt, Rinehart & Winston, in preparation.

Kohlberg, Lawrence, Ann Colby, John Gibbs, Betsy Speicher-Dubin, and Clark Power. "Assessing Moral Stages: A Manual." Cambridge: Center for Moral Education, Harvard University, 1978. Mimeo.

Kohlberg, Lawrence and Donald Elfenbein. "The Development of Moral Judgments Concerning Capital Punishment." *American Journal of Orthopsychiatry* (1975), 45:614–39.

Kohlberg, Lawrence, K. Kauffman, P. Scharf, and J. Hickey. "The Just Community Approach to Corrections: A Theory." *Journal of Moral Education* (1975), 4:243–60.

Kohlberg, Lawrence and Richard Kramer. "Continuities and Discontinuities in Childhood and Adult Moral Development." *Human Development* (1969), 12:93–120.

Kohlberg, Lawrence, Peter J. Scharf, and Joseph Hickey. "The Justice Structure of the Prison: A Theory and Intervention." *The Prison Journal* (Autumn-Winter 1972), pp. 3–14.

Kohlberg, Lawrence and Elliot Turiel. "Moral Development and Education," in *Collected Papers on Moral Development and Moral Education.* Edited by Lawrence Kohlberg. Cambridge: Center for Moral Education, Harvard University, 1973.

—— *Moralization: A Cognitive Developmental Approach to Socialization.* New York: Holt, Rinehart & Winston, in preparation.

Krebs, Dennis and Ali Rosenwald. "Moral Reasoning and Moral Behavior in Conventional Adults." *Merrill Palmer Quarterly* 23:(1977):77–87.

Krebs, Richard and Lawrence Kohlberg. "Moral Judgment and Ego Controls as Determinants of Resistance to Cheating." Cambridge: Center for Moral Education, Harvard University, 1973. Mimeo.

Kuhn, Deanna. "Short-Term Longitudinal Evidence for the Sequentiality of Kohlberg's Early Stages of Moral Judgment." *Developmental Psychology* (1976), 12:162–66.

Kuhn, Deanna, J. Langer, L. Kohlberg, and N. Haan. "The Development of Formal Operations in Logical and Moral Judgment." *Genetic Psychology Monographs* (1977), 95:97–188.

Kurdek, Lawrence A. "Perspective Taking As the Cognitive Basis of Children's Moral Development: A Review of the Literature." *Merrill Palmer Quarterly* (1978), 24:3–28.

Kurtines, William and Esther B. Grief. "The Development of Moral Thought: Review and Evaluation of Kohlberg's work." *Psychological Bulletin* (1974), 81:453–70.

Lickona, Thomas. "Piaget Misunderstood: A Critique of the Criticisms of Theory and Moral Development." *Merrill Palmer Quarterly* (1969), 16:337–50.

—— "Research on Piaget's Theory of Moral Development." In Thomas Lickona, ed., *Moral Development and Behavior: Theory, Research, and Social Issues*, pp. 219–40. New York: Holt, Rinehart & Winston, 1976.

Mead, George H. "Social Consciousness and the Consciousness of Meaning." In H. Standish Thayer, ed., *Pragmatism: The Classic Writings*, pp. 341–50. New York: New American Library, 1970.

Milgram, Stanley. *Obedience to Authority*. New York: Harper & Row, 1975.

Miller, Patricia H., Frank S. Kessel, and John H. Flavell. "Thinking About Thinking About People Thinking About . . .: A Study of Social Cognitive Development." *Child Development* (1970), 41:613–23.

Muss, Rolf E. "Kohlberg's Cognitive-Developmental Approach to Adolescent Morality." *Adolescence* (1976), 11:39–59.

Peters, R. S. "Moral Development: A Plea for Pluralism." In T. Mischel, ed., *Cognitive Development and Epistemology*, pp. 237–67. New York: Academic Press, 1971.

Peterson, Howard L. "The Quest for Moral Order." *Journal of Moral Education* (1974), 4:39–46.

Piaget, Jean. *The Language and Thought of the Child*. Translated by M. Gabain. Cleveland: Meridian Books, 1955. Originally published, 1923.

—— *The Moral Judgment of the Child*. Translated by M. Gabain. New York: The Free Press, 1965. Originally published, 1932.

—— "Intellectual Evolution from Adolescence to Adulthood." *Human Development* (1972), 15:1–12.

—— "Affective Unconscious and Cognitive Unconscious." In *The Child and Reality*, pp. 31–48. Edited by J. Piaget. Translated by A. Rosin. New York: Grossman, 1973.

—— *Structuralism*. Translated by C. Maschler. New York: Harper & Row, 1973.

—— *The Development of Thought: Equilibration of Cognitive Structures*. Translated by A. Rosin. New York: The Viking Press, 1975.

Piaget, Jean and Barbel Inhelder. *The Child's Conception of Space*. Translated by J. F. Langden and J. L. Lunzer. New York: Norton, 1967. Originally published, 1948.

—— *The Psychology of the Child*. Translated by H. Weaver. New York: Basic Books, 1969.

Puka, Bill. "Moral Education and Its Cure." In J. R. Meyer, ed., *Reflections on Values Education*, pp. 47–86. Ontario, Canada: Wilfried Laurier University Press, 1976.

Rawls, John. *A Theory of Justice*. Cambridge: Belknap Press, 1971.

Rest, James. "The Hierarchical Nature of Moral Judgment: A Study of Patterns of Comprehension and Preference of Moral Stages." Cambridge: Center for Moral Education, Harvard University. Mimeo.

Rest, James, Elliot Turiel and Lawrence Kohlberg. "Level of Moral Development As a Determinant of Preference and Comprehension of Moral Judgments Made by Others." *Journal of Personality* (1969), 37:225–52.

Selman, Robert L. "The Relation of Social Perspective Taking to Moral Development: Analytic and Empirical Approaches." Harvard Graduate School of Education, 1975. Mimeo.

—— "Social Cognitive Understanding: A Guide to Educational and Clinical Practice." In T. Lickona, ed., *Moral Development: Theory, Research, and Social Issues*, pp. 299–316. New York: Holt, Rinehart & Winston, 1976.

—— "Toward a Structural Analysis of Developing Interpersonal Relations Concepts: Research with Normal and Disturbed Preadolescent Boys." In Anne D. Pick, ed., *Minnesota Symposia on Child Psychology*, 10:156–93. Minneapolis: University of Minnesota Press, 1976.

Selman, Robert L. and William Damon. "The Necessity (but Insufficiency) of Social Perspective Taking for Conceptions of Justice at Three Early Levels." In David J. DePalma and Jeanne M. Foley, eds., *Moral Development: Current Theory and Research*, pp. 57–73. Hillsdale, N.J.: Erlbaum Associates, 1975.

Shantz, Carol V. "The Development of Social Cognition." In E. Marvis Hetherington, ed., *Review of Child Development Research*, 5:257–324. Chicago: University of Chicago Press, 1975.

Simpson, Elizabeth L. "Moral Development Research: A Case Study of Scientific Cultural Bias." *Human Development* (1974), 17:81–105.

Stuab, Erwin. "The Use of Role Playing and Induction in Children's Learning of Helping and Sharing Behaviors." *Child Development* (1971), 42:805–16.

Turiel, Elliot. "An Experimental Test of the Sequentiality of Developmental Stages in the Child's Moral Judgments." *Journal of Personality and Social Psychology* (1966), 3:611–18.

—— "Developmental Processes in the Child's Moral Thinking." In

P. H. Mussen, J. Langer, and M. Covington, eds., *Trends and Issues in Developmental Psychology,* pp. 92–133. New York: Holt, Rinehart & Winston, 1969.

—— "Stage Transition in Moral Development." In R. Travers, ed., *Second Handbook of Research in Teaching,* pp. 732–58. Chicago: Rand McNally, 1973.

Werner, Heinz. *Comparative Psychology of Mental Development.* Chicago: Follet, 1948.

# Name Index

# Subject Index